THE DARK CENTER

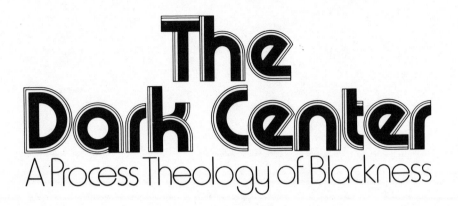

The Dark Center
A Process Theology of Blackness

Eulalio R. Baltazar

PAULIST PRESS
New York / Paramus / Toronto

Library of Congress
Catalog Card Number: 73-83811

ISBN 0-8091-1788-6

Cover Design: Daniel Pezza

Published by Paulist Press
Editorial Office: 1865 Broadway, N.Y., N.Y. 10023
Business Office: 400 Sette Drive, Paramus, N.J. 07652

Printed and bound in the
United States of America

ACKNOWLEDGMENTS

Grateful acknowledgment is made to the publishers listed below for their
permission to quote from the following works:

White over Black by Winthrop Jordan. Chapel Hill: University of North
Carolina Press and Institute of Early American History and Culture, ©
1968; quotes taken from the paperback edition by Penguin Books, Inc,
Baltimore, 1968. Reprinted with permission.

Mystical Theology of Dionysius the Areopagite. London: The Shrine of
Wisdom, 1923. Reprinted with permission.

"The New Testament Doctrine of Baptism" by David Stanley, in *Theological
Studies* 18 (1957). Reprinted with permission.

"The Significance of Skin Color in Human Relations" by Kenneth J. Gergen,
in *Color and Race*, ed. J. H. Franklin. Boston: Beacon Press, 1968.
Originally published in *Daedalus*, Color and Race, 1967. Copyright ©
1967 by American Academy of Arts and Sciences. Reprinted with
permission.

Sex and Race, I by J. A. Rogers. New York: Helga M. Rogers, 9th edition.
Copyright © 1967. Reprinted with permission.

Depth Psychology and a New Ethic, by Erich Neumann, trans. by Eugene
Rolfe. New York: G. P. Putnam's Sons, copyright © 1969. Reprinted with
permission.

Sleepy-Time Stories by Maud Ballington Booth. New York: G. P. Putnam's
Sons, 1899. Reprinted with permission.

CONTENTS

INTRODUCTION

While the practical orientation of this book is the understanding of the philosophic and religious roots of racism in the West, the importance of a theology of blackness goes beyond the problem of racism. It affects the very approach to theology itself. For the past two thousand years, Western rational theology influenced by the Hellenic philosophic ideal of lucidity, clarity of form, and explicit statement and definition has been fleeing from the mythical and mystical as being vague, inexact, undefinable and as being unsusceptible to formulation and systematization. It was a theology that attempted to be "scientific" instead of being "mystical." In short, rational theology was a theology of light rather than a theology of darkness. Its analogue for knowledge is sight rather than hearing; its object is "form" rather than "symbol."

A theology of blackness attempts to show that knowledge in the scriptures is through hearing rather than sight. Its wisdom is not conventional wisdom or the wisdom of common sense which is what Hellenic philosophy provides. Its wisdom is foolishness to men, hence, it is appropriately symbolized as darkness. White theology has translated the truths

1

of scriptures in terms of the categories of conventional wisdom. God, for example, is presented as Being instead of non-Being, as Presence instead of a Deus Absconditus, as "I am who am" instead of an "I will be who I will be." The whole of conventional theology is built on conceptual reason as man's highest faculty, hence, it is a rational theology, instead of on imagination which, from a different epistemological perspective, could be superior to reason,[1] hence theology as mystery. In conventional wisdom, reason is symbolized as light (white) while imagination is symbolized as dark (black). But we need to adopt a new thought pattern to see that what common sense considers as negative could be positive. With a processive thought pattern it is hoped that modern theology can recover its roots in the darkness of mystery and myth and thus rescue itself from its rootlessness in rationalism and demythologization in its effort to become scientific and be in vogue.

A theology of blackness symbolizes the Supreme Realty as Divine Darkness and Faith as a saving darkness. The Christian dialectic is from the light of reason (conventional wisdom) to the darkness of faith as mystery. But more of this later.

The work is divided into two main parts. The first part deals with the white theology [2] of blackness. In the first chapter, the scriptural passages upon which the white theology of blackness is based are presented. Then a survey of the implication of this white theology of blackness in human relations is shown. First of all, the transference of the theological symbolism to skin color is described (chapter 2), then the secularization of the religious symbolism is noted (chapter 3), and finally the psychological effects of the Western symbolism of color on both whites and blacks brought up in Western culture are outlined.

In the second part of the study a processive theology of blackness is attempted. As prelude to this second part, the efforts of some black religious thinkers to offset and counteract the Western color symbolism is briefly noted. But in these efforts the dualistic thought pattern operative in white theology is also operative in black theology such that black is now made to symbolize the positive and white the negative which in effect is nothing but reverse symbolism and racism. The dualistic thought pattern is laid aside as inadequate and a new thought pattern which is processive is introduced. From this new thought pattern we propose a new symbolism for black and white which we believe to be more in conformity with the ambivalent values of black and white as found in various cultures (chapter 5), in mythic and ordinary experience (chapter 6), in philosophic thought as dynamic and evolutionary (chapter 7) and in the scriptures themselves (chapter 8). Finally, a processive theology of blackness or darkness is sketched in the last chapter.

Darkness is the source of life and energy at all levels of being. As the source of green life is a dark soil and as the source of light energy is the dark center of the sun, so the source of life for theology is the darkness of mystery and myth and the source of the life of grace for Christians is the saving darkness of faith which hides the Divine Darkness. But both Western theology and the Christian life have undergone a bleaching process, driven by the fear of their respective dark centers.

When theology has made peace with the positive darkness of mystery which is its inner depth, then it is able to exert power and influence in a world tending toward full-blown secularism. And when Christians begin to accept blackness as the unique symbol of the Christian life, then they could begin to exercise their vocation as peacemakers in the world. Without the acceptance of positive darkness there is only self-alienation and the projection of this alienation in the world.

It is hoped that this work will help, albeit in a small way, toward peace in the world today.

1

THE RELIGIOUS BASIS
OF WESTERN
COLOR SYMBOLISM

Before we launch into the study of the Western color symbolism of black and white, perhaps it is necessary to consider color symbolism in general.

Colors convey meaning. Thus, they belong to the semantic and epistemological realms. Now meaning can be conveyed denotatively or connotatively. A denotative meaning is expressed by words that refer to specific objects or events. For example, the word *smoke* refers directly to the gaseous object which results from burning. But the same word suggests, indicates or symbolizes along with, or in addition to the explicit and recognized meaning, another meaning, as in this instance, that of fire. Hence, the term smoke has also a connotative meaning. Symbols and signs are connotative in meaning. They point not to themselves (denotative) but beyond themselves (connotative). Symbols differ from signs in that they participate in the thing symbolized while signs do not. Religious symbols, for example, participate in the reality they symbolize. Thus, Christ as the supreme Christian symbol not only points beyond to the Godhead but also participates in the Godhead. A sign, on the other hand, such as a national flag, while pointing beyond itself to the ideals and aspirations of a nation, does not however participate in the reality it signifies; in itself a flag is just a piece of cloth.

Colors have both a denotative and a connotative meaning. Color at the denotative level is neutral. Color is just color, that is, a physical and optic phenomenon. As Webster's Dictionary defines it, it is a "sensation evoked as a response to the stimulation of the eye and its attached nervous mechanisms by radiant energy of certain wave lengths and intensities." At the denotative level the knowing subject is not involved personally. His emotions do not come into play.

At the connotative level, colors become the center and focus of passionate sentiments and values and, depending on the color, elicit particular types of feelings or emotions toward oneself and others. In the realm of advertising, the connotative significance of color has been used by advertisers, architects, interior designers, and artists to great advantage.

Color at the connotative level can be either a sign or a symbol. As a sign we have the example of the color green or red as traffic signs, green signifying "go ahead" and red, "stop." As a symbol, the color black, for example, is seen in the West as connoting evil, sin, ignorance, such that those who are possessed of black or dark skins participate in the reality which the color symbolizes, hence, in evil, sin, ignorance and so on; conversely, white as symbol connotes goodness, salvation, beauty, and other positive values such that those possessed of fair or white skins participate in these positive values.

It is obvious that our interest in color is with its connotative and symbolic aspect.

Let us first briefly indicate the various connotative meanings of the colors black and white in the Western tradition before we examine its beginnings or sources.

From a careful study of color symbolism in the Western cultural and literary tradition, Matthew Luckiesh observes that black is commonly associated with woe, gloom, darkness, dread, death, terror, wickedness, curse, mourning, and mortification. And from a study by Walter Sargent may be added the attributes of defilement, error and annihilation. From the studies of Faber Birren, the major association elicited by black is despair.[1] In contrast to the above negative meanings of the color black are positive meanings associated with the color white, namely, triumph, light, innocence, joy, divine power, purity, regeneration, happiness, gaiety, peace, chastity, truth, modesty, femininity, and delicacy. These studies based on several direct and well-controlled tests convincingly demonstrate not only that white is rated more positively than black, but that both Negroes as well as whites feel similarly in this regard.[2]

Western color symbolism permeates all Western languages both sacred and profane. As Howard Thurman notes: "The identification of blackness with evil, with the ominous, the destructive, the terrifying, is all through the language both sacred and profane. Black magic is evil; so is a black crime, but a white lie is acceptable." [3]

A question at this point is the source of this Western color symbolism. To say that it arose as a justification for the political, economic and social inequalities between blacks and whites, is, as we noted in the preface of this study, to put the cart before the horse, for even before colonialism and its effects of exploitation of blacks, Western color symbolism was well established.

We affirmed earlier that the main source is religious and mythological. This is what we hope to substantiate in this chapter. P. J. Heather notes that one of the sources for Western color symbolism is Greek mythology as found in Greek literature.[4] He notes that in Euripides mention is made of "black-robed ruler of the dead" and in Virgil the black

Styx has a similar symbolism as the appropriate hue for the dead.[5] In Homer black is applied to death, destiny and pangs, while the Greek tragedians apply the epithet black to the Furies, Tartarus, the heart and mind, Hades, and Erebus.[6]

By way of contrast, Heather notes that the color white is more highly esteemed than the color black: [7]

> In the Greek and Latin classics the epithet "white-armed" applied by Homer in the *Odyssey* to Nausicaa and to Arete, and in the *Iliad* to Hero; clothing and light of this colour in the works of Sophocles and Euripides; Virgil's use of the adjective "candidus" for Alexis, Nais, Dido, Venus, and of "niveus" for Palla and for the arms of the goddess Venus add further support to the idea of the high esteem attached to whiteness.

Granted the influence of Greek literature and culture on Western color symbolism, by far the more influential and pervading sources are white Christianity and white theology. Many writers concerned with the origin of Western color symbolism attest to the fact. Thus, Harold Isaacs notes that "these concepts and usages of black evil and white goodness, of beautiful fairness and ugly blackness, are deeply imbedded in the Bible, are folded into the language of Milton and Shakespeare, indeed are laced into almost every entwining strand of the art and literature in which our history is clothed." [8]

Thurman notes how the white Christian religion identifies black with the negative and white with the positive: [9]

> In a religion such as Christianity, the image of God in the minds of many Christians is that of a kindly, benevolent, bewhiskered white man, seated on a white-throne, surrounded by blond and brunette angels who

stand ready to serve Him in praises or as messengers. The Devil, on the other hand, is the Prince of Darkness while the imps of the Devil are black. Hence the phrase "black as imp." Now this is strong medicine even for the pure of heart. What a vote of confidence it must have been to a white person to feel that the Creator of the Universe was made in his image. Of course, there is nothing universal about the notion that God is imaged in accordance with the ideal of the beholder. The advantage is obvious.

Roger Bastide also notes the black-white antithesis inherent in white Christianity: [10]

White is used to express the pure, while black expresses the diabolical. The conflict between Christ and Satan, the spiritual and the carnal, good and evil came finally to be expressed by the conflict between white and black, which underlines and synthesizes all others. Even the blind, who know only night, think of a swarm of angels or of devils in association with white and black—for example, "a black soul," "the blackness of an action," "a dark deed," "the innocent whiteness of the lily," "the candor of a child," "to bleach someone of a crime." These are not merely adjectives and nouns. Whiteness brings to mind the light, ascension into the bright realm, the immaculateness of virgin snow, the white dove of the Holy Spirit, the transparency of limpid air; blackness suggests the infernal streams of the bowels of the earth, the pit of hell, the devil's color.

The basis for the black-white antithesis in white Christianity is white theology. In his source book on bible themes, Thierry Maertens sums up the meaning and symbolism of black and white, night and day, darkness and light, as generally understood by white theology: [11]

> Darkness was the night with all its scourges. Light was day, holiness and life with God. It was necessary therefore to pass from darkness to light, to emerge from the darkness of Egypt and to enter the path of light. This was a call for a strict moral life in fraternal charity by the imitation of God, who is light.
> This call was to mark the whole of Christian ethics, which are rooted in the death and resurrection of the Savior, our paschal light; hence, the baptismal context of the principal passages of the Epistles. Hence also the struggle between light and darkness in St. John; Jesus was the light of the world, and His presence forced one to choose between Him and the darkness.

Thus, one can see from the foregoing description of the black-white color symbolism in white theology that it touches the very depth and meaning of the Christian life. Black or darkness stands for all that is opposed to Christ. Following Christ is choosing light over darkness.

But let us now go directly to the scriptures and reexamine the passages upon which the black-white color symbolism of white theology is based.[12]

In the scriptures, the black-white symbolism is variously expressed as darkness-light or night-day correlatives. It is also expressed antithetically by various opposed images such as sunny as opposed to cloudy, brightness as opposed to the presence of a shadow, and so on. We might note too that where one set of correlatives is used, the others are usually implied. Let us choose a passage in which the color black is taken as a negative symbol to illustrate the point:

Distressed and starving he will wander through the
   country
and, starving, he will become frenzied,
blaspheming his king and his God;
turning his gaze upward,
then down to earth,
he will find only distress and darkness,
the blackness of anguish,
and will see nothing but night.
Is not all blackness where anguish is? Isa. 8:21-23.

Thus, darkness, blackness, night are used interchangeably to express negative values. But let us attempt as far as possible to discuss each set of correlatives separately. Let us first examine the light-darkness antithesis.

The light-darkness antithesis is first of all used in the most sweeping or metaphysical sense to symbolize being and existence, on the one hand, and nonbeing or chaos, on the other. Thus, the opening words of the scriptures, from the point of view of white theology, sets the scene for the conflict between light and darkness:

In the beginning
God created the heavens and the earth.
Now the earth was a formless void,
there was darkness over the deep,
and God's spirit hovered over the water.
God said, "Let there be light,"
and there was light.
God saw that light was good,
and God divided light from darkness.
God called light "day,"
and darkness he called "night."   Gen. 1:1-5.

We notice the identification of light with the good in the passage. Goodness in the context is understood to mean metaphysical goodness, that is, the possession of being or existence, not necessarily moral goodness. Light as something physical is physically and metaphysically good. Darkness as a physical fact, on the other hand, is physically bad. Thus, it is used by God as a form and sign of physical punishment:[13]

> Then Yahweh said to Moses, "Stretch out your hand towards heaven, and let darkness, darkness so thick that it can be felt, cover the land of Egypt." So Moses stretched out his hand toward heaven, and for three days there was deep darkness over the whole land of Egypt. No one could see anyone else or move about for three days, but where the sons of Israel lived there was light for them.   Ex. 10:21-23.

Notice further in the above passage that physical darkness and light given as a punishment or a reward are merely of a temporary character. But it will later be considered an abiding condition of Egypt and Israel as can be seen in the following passage where there is an identification, or, at least, an affinity in the character of the peoples with physical light and darkness:

> When impious men imagined they had the holy nation
>   in their power,
> they themselves lay prisoners of the dark, in the fetters
>   of long night,
> confined under their own roofs, banished from eternal
>   providence.
> While they thought to remain unnoticed with their secret
>   sins,

curtained by dark forgetfulness,
they were scattered (plunged in darkness) [14] in fearful
  dismay,
terrified by apparitions.
The hiding place sheltering them could not ward off
  their fear;
terrifying noises echoed round them;
and gloomy, grim-faced spectres haunted them.
No fire had power enough to give them light,
nor could the brightly blazing stars
illuminate that dreadful night—   Wisdom 17:2-5.

In contrast to the previous passage which describes the
abiding condition of Egypt, is the following passage which
describes the lot of Israel:

But for your holy ones all was great light.
The Egyptians who could hear their voices, though not
  see their shapes,
called them fortunate because they had not suffered too;
they thanked them for doing no injury in return for
  previous wrongs
and asked forgiveness for their past ill-will.
In contrast to the darkness, you gave your people a pillar
  of blazing fire,
to guide them on their unknown journey,
a mild sun for their ambitious migration.
But well they deserved, those others, to be deprived of
  light and imprisoned in darkness,
for having kept in captivity your children,
by whom the imperishable light of the Law was to be
  given to the world.   Wisdom 18:1-4.

Notice the last sentence of the previous passage. Already

there is an advance in symbolism from the physical to the moral level. Where before, light and darkness symbolized physical conditions of peoples, now they are also used to symbolize moral condition. There is a transference of the physical cycle of light and darkness to the moral realm. Light is used to symbolize law and wisdom; darkness to symbolize the path of sin: We can observe this symbolism at the moral level in the following passages: [15]

The path of the virtuous is like the light of dawn,
its brightness growing to the fullness of day;
the way of the wicked is as dark as night,
they cannot tell what it is they stumble over.

Prov. 4:18-19.

So justice is removed far away from us,
and integrity keeps its distance.
We looked for light and all is darkness,
for brightness and we walk in the dark.   Isa. 59:9-10.

Some were living in darkness,
fettered in misery and irons
for defying the orders of God, . . .

Then they called to Yahweh in their trouble
and he rescued them from their sufferings;
releasing them from gloom and darkness,
shattering their chains.   Ps. 106:10,13.

In the New Testament, a single but most influential passage will suffice to show the light-dark symbolism at the moral level:

On these grounds is sentence pronounced:
that though the light has come into the world

men have shown they prefer
darkness to the light
because their deeds were evil.
And indeed, everybody who does wrong
hates the light and avoids it,
for fear his actions should be exposed;
but the man who lives by the truth
comes out into the light,
so that it may be plainly seen that what he does is done
    in God.   John 3:19-21.

At the moral level, in general, light is associated with what is morally good and darkness with what is morally evil. But more specifically, light is also associated with love, charity, while darkness is associated with hate; light is a sign of moral conversion or illumination, while darkness is a sign of obduracy and reprobation. We note these specific symbolisms, for example:

Anyone who claims to be in the light
but hates his brother
is still in the dark.
But anyone who loves his brother is living in the light
and need not be afraid of stumbling;
unlike the man who hates his brother and is in the
    darkness,
not knowing where he is going,
because it is too dark to see.   1 John 2:9-11.

Thus, in the above passage, light is associated with love, charity.[16] Light is also associated with conversion as illumination: [17]

I shall deliver you from the people and from the pagans,
to whom I am sending you to open their eyes, so that

they may turn from darkness to light, from the dominion
of Satan to God . . .   Acts 16:17-18.

Notice in the last passage the association of light with the
domain of Satan. Thus, the separation of light and darkness
made in the beginning by God is now made specific in a
moral sense. The ways of light or of darkness are now the
kingdoms of Jesus or of Satan: [18]

> Light and darkness have nothing in common.
> Christ is not the ally of Belial,
> nor has a believer anything to share with an unbeliever.
> 2 Cor. 6:14-15.

> . . . thanking the Father who has made it possible for
> you to join the saints and with them to inherit the light.
> Because that is what he has done: he has taken us out
> of the power of darkness and created a place for us in
> the kingdom of the Son he loves . . .   Col. 1:12-13.

We observe that where, before, light was associated with a
people, Israel, and darkness with Egypt, now, light is associated with the personification of a people. There is a special
application of the symbol of light to Christ as the Light.
Christ was not merely to bring light, he himself was the light,
for he was the exemplar of the union between man and God
who is the creator of the Kingdom of Light. For example, in
the following passage note the association:

> In the beginning was the Word:
> the Word was with God
> and the Word was God.
> He was with God in the beginning.
> Through him all things came to be,

not one thing had its being but through him.
All that came to be had life in him
and that life was the light of men,
a light that shines in the dark,
a light that darkness could not overpower.

A man came, sent by God.
His name was John.
He came as a witness,
as a witness to speak for the light,
so that everyone might believe through him.
He was not the light,
only a witness to speak for the light.

The Word was the true light
that enlightens all men;
and he was coming into the world.
He was in the world
that had its being through him,
and the world did not know him.
He came to his own domain
and his own people did not accept him.
But to all who did accept him
he gave power to become children of God,
to all who believe in the name of him
who was born not out of human stock
or urge of the flesh
or will of man
but of God himself.
The Word was made flesh,
he lived among us,
and we saw his glory,
the glory that is his as the only Son of the Father,
full of grace and truth.   John 1:1-14.

Here in this famous prologue of John's Gospel, we have the identification of light itself with the Word of God who is Christ, the Messiah. And Jesus himself spoke of himself as light: [19]

I am the light of the world;
anyone who follows me will not be walking in the dark;
he will have the light of life.   John 8:12.

Thus, one has to change paths, walk toward God's light and not remain a son of darkness. Since the coming of Christ-light, a choice has to be made. A judgment was made upon darkness:

Besides, you know the "time" has come: you must wake up now: our salvation is even nearer than it was when we were converted. The night is almost over, it will be daylight soon—let us give up all the things we prefer to do under cover of the dark; let us arm ourselves and appear in the light. Let us live decently as people do in the daytime: no drunken orgies, no promiscuity or licentiousness, and no wrangling or jealousy. Let your armour be the Lord Jesus Christ; forget about satisfying your bodies with all their cravings.
                                        Rom. 13:11-14.[20]

To be in the light was to have knowledge, to have darkness, ignorance, both intellectual and moral blindness: [21]

If our gospel does not penetrate the veil, then the veil is on those who are not on the way to salvation; the unbelievers whose minds the god of this world has blinded, to stop them seeing the light shed by the Good News of the glory of Christ, who is the image of God. For it is

not ourselves that we are preaching, but Christ Jesus as
the Lord, and ourselves as your servants for Jesus' sake.
It is the same God that said, 'Let there be light shining
out of darkness', who has shone in our minds to radiate
the light of the knowledge of God's glory, the glory on
the face of Christ.   2 Cor. 4:3-6.

Those who refused the light would be thrown into outer
darkness: [22]

When the king came in to look at the guests he noticed
one man who was not wearing a wedding garment, and
said to him, "How did you get in here, my friend, without a wedding garment?" And the man was silent. Then
the king said to the attendants, "Bind him hand and
foot and throw him out into the dark, where there will
be weeping and grinding of teeth." For many are called,
but few are chosen.   Matt. 22:11-14.

Finally, the light-darkness symbolism is used in an eschatological sense to symbolize the final victory of the reign of
light and the defeat of darkness forever. There would be an
everlasting light for the heavenly Jerusalem:

I saw that there was no temple in the city since the
Lord God Almighty and the Lamb were themselves the
temple, and the city did not need the sun or the moon
for light, since it was lit by the radiant glory of God and
the Lamb was a lighted torch for it. The pagan nations
will live by its light and the kings of the earth will bring
it their treasures. The gates of it will never be shut by
day—and there will be no night there.
                              Rev. 21:22-26.[23]

Having been given this epic symbolism of light-darkness, Christians are now exhorted to behave as sons of light rather than as sons of darkness:

> But it is not as if you live in the dark, my brothers, for that Day to overtake you like a thief. No, you are all sons of light and sons of the day: we do not belong to the night or to darkness, so we should not go on sleeping, as everyone else does, but stay wide awake and sober. Night is the time for sleepers to sleep and drunkards to be drunk, but we belong to the day and we should be sober. Rom. 4:4-8.

St. Paul in the above passage also uses night and day as symbols, one negative, the other positive. Hence, let us also study the closely related symbols of night and day.

Night was a sign of God's anger. Should God's anger be aroused the regular rhythm of night and day which was a sign of God's fidelity was shattered and day turned into night:

> Trouble for those who are waiting so longingly for the
>   day of Yahweh!
> What will this day of Yahweh mean for you?
> It will mean darkness, not light. Amos 5:18.

> That day—it is the Lord Yahweh who speaks—
> I will make the sun go down at noon,
> and darken the earth in broad daylight. Amos 8:9.

> The day of Yahweh is coming, merciless,
> with wrath and fierce anger,
> to reduce the earth to desert
> and root out the sinners from it.
> For the stars of the sky and Orion

shall not let their light shine;
the sun shall be dark when it rises,
and the moon not shed her light.   Isa. 13:9-10.[24]

Night was the time for attacking a town:

Joshua prepared to march against Ai with all the fighting men. He chose thirty thousand men from among the
bravest and sent them out by night . . .   Jos. 8:3.

He (Zebul the governor) sent messengers to Abimelech at Aruhah, bidding them tell him, 'Listen! Gaal
son of Ebed has come to Shechem with his brothers
and they are stirring up the town against you. Move,
therefore, under cover of dark, you and the men you
have with you, and take up concealed positions in the
countryside.'   Judges 9:31-32.

Night was the time the angel of death was active (4 Kings
29:25). It was the time symbolic of evil: (Job 24:14; 27:20;
30:17; Isa. 15:1, 21:11-12). It was also the time given over
to tears: [25]

I am worn out with groaning,
every night I drench my pillow
and soak my bed with tears;
my eye is wasted with grief,
I have grown old with enemies all round me.
                                        Ps. 6:6-7.

It was at night that Christ was taken captive (Matt.
26:3-34; 1 Cor. 11:23). Thenceforth for *John* night was
the symbol of evil and sin:

As soon as Judas had taken the piece of bread he went out.
Night had fallen.   John 13:30.

Are there not twelve hours in the day?
A man can walk in the daytime without stumbling
because he has the light of this world to see by;
but if he walks at night he stumbles,
because there is no light to guide him.
                                    John 11:10.[26]

Evening and "bed time" often spelled trials and evil. Death was represented as a long sleep.[27] Dawn and "waking" by contrast were signs of safety, the time of God's bounty: [28]

His (Yahweh's) anger lasts a moment, his favour a life-time;
in the evening, a spell of tears, but in the morning, shouts of joy.   Ps. 29:6.

God is inside the city, she can never fall,
at the crack of dawn God helps her;   Ps. 45:6.

Waking might also be a veiled allusion to the resurrection: [29]

Blessed is he who stands firm and attains a thousand three hundred and thirty-five days. But you go away and rest; and you will rise for your share at the end of time.   Dan. 12:2.

Night had been vanquished by the vigil of the Passover: [30] The pillar of light proved to the people God's conquest of the night: [31]

Yahweh went before them, by day in the form of a pillar

of cloud to show them the way, and by night in the form of a pillar of fire to give them light.   Ex. 13:21.

Associated with the terms night and day are the terms black and white. In the scriptures, white symbolizes purity, sinlessness, grace and glory. Thus, Psalm 51:7 says, "Wash me, and I shall be whiter than snow." [32] Again, white garments are symbolic of divine favor, of the purity of one's soul. Thus, "Let thy garments be always white." [33] What is true in the Old Testament is repeated in the New. In Matthew 9:3 in Christ's transfiguration, it is said: "His raiment became shining, exceeding white as snow." Good angels are dressed in white. Thus, Magdalen "saw two angels in white" (John 20:12), or, again, "two men stood by them (the women) in white robes" (Acts 1:10), or as Mark 16:5 notes: "Entering into the sepulchre, they saw a young man sitting on the right side, clothed in a long white garment." Finally, the symbolism of white as signifying purity, sinlessness and the fullness of grace is fulfilled and consummated in heaven. As John portrays the Kingdom of Light, the Son of Man is described as follows: "His head and his hair were white as white wool, and as snow" (Rev. 1:14). And the elect in heaven are garbed in white robes (Rev. 7:9) before a great white throne (Rev. 20:11).[34]

In contrast to the symbolism of whiteness as positive, blackness is used as a sign of sin and damnation. Thus, "My skin is black upon me, and my bones are burned with heat (Job 30:30); "I clothe the heavens with blackness, and I make sackcloth their covering" (Isa. 50:3); "All faces shall gather blackness" (Joel 2:6); and, finally, just as whiteness is a symbol of the heavenly, so blackness is a symbol of hell which is "the blackness of darkness forever" (Jude 13).[35] Black is also a symbol of mourning [36] and is the symbolic effect of famine and wounds.[37]

A related symbol of blackness is that of the shadow.

Shadow implies unreality, transitoriness, misfortune, death. Thus, in Job 8:9, it is said that "our days on earth are a shadow." [38] Again, "all my members are like a shadow" (Job 17:7); misfortune is compared to "the valley of the shadow of death" (Ps. 23:4) or, "in darkness and in the shadow of death" (Lk. 1:79). In contrast to our life on earth as a shadow, is the kingdom of light and the Father of lights from whom every good gift and every perfect gift comes and in whom is no variableness, nor shadow of turning (Jas. 1:17).

2

TRANSFERENCE OF THE RELIGIOUS SYMBOLISM TO SKIN COLOR

During the Middle Ages and prior to it, the black-white color symbolism derived from the scriptures was not transferred to skin color. There was no racism then, despite the mutual exclusivity and polarity of the colors black and white. Does this mean that during the Middle Ages there were no dark-skinned peoples known by the medieval Christians to whom they could transfer their religious color symbolism of black and white? This supposition is contradicted by the fact that before and during the Middle Ages white Christians were aware of black Christians, Moors and other dark-skinned peoples like the Ethiopians. Could the reason for the absence of racism be that the dark-skinned Africans the white Christians knew were of a lighter color than the sub-Saharan Africans and therefore did not arouse as much shock and emotional reaction as the darker West Africans? But this explanation for the absence of racism during the Middle Ages is also wrong since it has been estimated that "during the Middle Ages, at least twenty thousand blacks were sent each year from West Africa into North Africa, or at least two million per century." [1]

Historically we know that racism arose at the time the Europeans started the colonization and enslavement process of the West Africans.[2] Hence, the popular explanation for the cause of racism is the need to justify the radical economic difference between the European and the African. In other words, the values attributed to the colors black and white were a product of the radical economic difference separating whites and blacks. But this explanation is incorrect for even prior to colonialism, the concept of black and white was well established. As Winthrop Jordan reminds us, "Long before they found that some men were black, Englishmen found in the idea of blackness a way of expressing some of their most ingrained values. No other color except white conveyed so much emotional impact." [3] According to the Oxford English Dictionary, *black* before the sixteenth century meant "deeply stained with dirt; soiled, dirty, foul. . . . Having dark or deadly purposes, malignant; pertaining to or involving death, deadly; baneful, disastrous, sinister. . . . Foul, iniquitous, atrocious, horrible, wicked. . . . Indicating disgrace, censure, liability to punishment, etc." [4] To the English before the sixteenth century, black and white implied opposition, "beinge coloures utterlye contrary." [5] It denoted polarization: [6]

> Everye white will have its blacke,
> And everye sweete its sowre.

Jordan concludes that for the English, "white and black connoted purity and filthiness, virginity and sin, virtue and baseness, beauty and ugliness, beneficence and evil, God and the devil." [7]

The need to justify the economic dominance of the European over the black African is not a sufficient explanation for the origin of white racism for even before the age of colonialism, the position of blacks was economically lower than that of whites being employed as domestic servants, concubines, artisans, porters.[8] True, there is quite a difference between the "slave relationship of the Negro in the modern Western world" compared to that of the Middle Ages;[9] for the modern slave relationship is "always closely linked to the plantation system—the exploitation of large numbers of unskilled slave laborers in vast agricultural projects."[10] But granting the radical difference of the economic situation of the post-medieval period to the medieval one, still the colonialism of the post-medieval period is not a sufficient justification for the transference of the color symbolism to skin color, nor is it the cause of modern white racism if there did not first take place at the ideational level a more fundamental change, i.e., a change in the philosophic and theological consciousness of the West, occasioned by the Protestant Reformation and the Cartesian Revolution. Even if (by an impossible supposition) the colonial situation were present in the Middle Ages, still racism as the transference of the color symbolism to skin color would not have taken place without a change in the theological and philosophic consciousness of the age. Let me explain the point.

The medieval age in its theology and philosophy was both Platonic and Aristotelian since the two great thinkers of the age, St. Augustine and St. Thomas Aquinas, were influenced respectively by Plato and Aristotle. Now, the theological and philosophic anthropology of the medieval age was metaphysical. This means that the spiritual and transcendental was of greater value than the material and temporal. Accordingly, man was more his soul than his body. When preachers spoke of salvation, it was the salvation of souls that they talked about, not the salvation of the body. The soul was the form of the body. As form was superior to matter, giving it its essence or meaning, so the soul was superior to the body.

Because of this orientation toward the soul as opposed to that of the body, the symbolism of black and white was understandably and logically related to the soul and its condition. Thus, the soul was spoken of as white when it was in a state of grace, that is, when it was without sin, and spoken of as black when it was in a state of mortal or grievous sin. In the liturgy of baptism, this symbolism is apparent. Thus, the catechumen is robed in white to symbolize the spotless condition of the soul washed by the saving waters of baptism and the blood of Christ from its darkness and blackness both intellectual and moral. He is given a candle to symbolize the light of faith, of Christ, so that from henceforth the soul does not walk in darkness but by the light of faith.

Now, what about the body? In Plato, man was his soul. The body was a prison. In Aristotle, as modified by St. Thomas, the body was a cosubstantial principle. Man was composed substantially of body and soul. In terms of the Aristotelian categories of substance and accident, the color and shape and form of the body were not essential to being a man but rather were accidental, that is, nonessential. It was for this philosophic reason, it would seem, that the medieval white Christian did not make much of skin color. To him, it was not crucial or essential to being a man, that is, a Christian. What was essential was the whiteness of the soul. This metaphysical attitude would seem to explain also the presence of Black Christs and Black Madonnas in the Middle Ages who were glorified and prayed to. The symbolism then of black and white was in accordance with the metaphysical outlook of the age, hence used to symbolize the metaphysical, that is, the condition of the soul. Transference to skin color could not have been possible without also a change in the metaphysical outlook.

The change, as those knowledgeable in philosophy would

tell us, came even before Descartes when the realism of the Middle Ages gave way to the nominalism of William of Occam. But it was Descartes who, divorcing philosophy from its ancillary status to theology, gave the final impetus for a change in the philosophic and theological outlooks from the metaphysical to the empirical. Classical empiricism reached its full expression with the trio of English philosophers, Locke, Berkeley and Hume. With empiricism, not substances, universals, essences but phenomena, images, sense impressions became the object of knowledge. For Locke, substance was unknowable; for Berkeley, there was no substrate of substance as the foundation for qualities as ideas, and for Hume, man was a bundle of perception, that is, sense impressions. And finally, Kant, influenced by empiricism, accepted the view that all that the human mind can know are phenomena. Because of this change of epistemological outlook, observation was emphasized and to a lesser degree, scientific experimentation. And, if, as Hume asserts, man is a bundle of perceptions, it is only a short step to saying that man is his appearance, or man is as he appears. It was this new anthropology that facilitated the transference of the color symbolism from the soul to the body. The color symbolism thus came to be applied empirically rather than metaphysically. But even this transference would have remained purely in theory and not in fact if the economic colonization of Africans and the need to justify slavery were not present as reenforcing factors. In other words, the economic superiority and dominance of the Europeans confirmed their belief in the positive theological values attached to white skin and, conversely, the negative theological values attached to peoples with dark skins. The color symbolism which was previously applied to the condition of man's soul now came to be applied to a man's skin and this latter symbolism was reenforced by the economic difference between whites and blacks.

Let us take the English as an example of how the color symbolism of black and white came to be transferred to skin-color. English voyagers following the lead of Portugal and Spain came to realize that overseas exploration and plantations brought wealth, power, glory to the homeland. By the year 1550, English voyagers touched upon the shores of West Africa.[11] To them, "the most arresting characteristic of the newly discovered African was his color." "Indeed," observes Jordan, "when describing Negroes they frequently began with complexion and then moved on to dress."[12] Thus, the color of the Negro was the feature that produced the most powerful impact and it was partly owing to the suddenness of contact.[13] It might be added, however, that the color of the skin would not have produced such an impact if the consciousness of the English discoverers were not already oriented to the appearance as of capital importance in differentiating peoples.

As might be expected, explanations were sought as to the origin of the Negro's color. Natural explanations such as that the darkness of the skin is caused by the sun and that therefore those who lived in the tropics were dark while those that lived in northern regions were fair were given. But these explanations were discredited when it was found that *Americans* and *East-Indians* inhabiting northern climates were not black.[14] An alternative explanation was sought from the scriptures in terms of the color symbolism. The story of Ham's curse and all his descendants was considered entirely sufficient to account for the Negro's color and this explanation became relatively common in the seventeenth century.[15] According to the story in Genesis 9 and 10, Ham, after the Flood, had stared upon his father's (Noah) nakedness as he lay drunk in his tent, whereas Shem and Japheth, the other two sons, had covered their father without looking upon him. When Noah awoke, he cursed Canaan, son of

Ham, saying that he would be a slave unto his brothers. Jordan correctly observes that this text was used by the great church fathers such as St. Jerome and St. Augustine, but in order to explain slavery not black skin color. How then did the post-medieval Christian writers come to use this text to justify the origin of black skin color? According to Jordan, it was through contact with Jewish writings during the late medieval and renaissance years that made the Christians aware that *"Ham* originally connoted both "dark" and "hot." From the Talmudic and Midrashic sources was the suggestion "that 'Ham was smitten in his skin,' that Noah told Ham 'your seed will be ugly and dark-skinned,' and that Ham was father 'of Canaan who brought curses into the world, of Canaan who was cursed, of Canaan who darkened the faces of mankind,' of Canaan 'the notorious world-darkener.' " [16] Thus, as Jordan notes, the transference of the color symbolism to skin color "came during the sixteenth century—the first great century of overseas exploration." [17]

The transference of the theological color symbolism to skin color affected not only Protestants but also Catholics. The reason was partly due to the fact that the empirical outlook exercised a very broad influence on post-medieval man such that with justice we could call the age an age of renaissance affecting all Christians. The color symbolism made to justify first economic dominance and slavery also affected the domain of theology itself.

Let us consider how the color symbolism affected theology and religious practice. Thus, in line with the attitude that the appearance or phenomenal was important, color became important in depicting Christ, Mary and the saints. The colors black and white became so dominant that they dragged other colors along with them. For example, in painting the cloak of the Immaculate Virgin, celestial blue became a simple satellite of white, for they refer to the bright sky above, while dark colors refer to the underworld. Accordingly, the red flames of hell became associated with the darkest colors.[18]

An even more significant influence of the color symbolism was the operative process of deliberately whitening or bleaching the center of the Christian Faith, namely, Jesus Christ, from a Semitic to an Aryan person to which the entire history of Western painting bears witness. Both Aryans and Gentiles, even the most anti-Semitic, worship their God incarnated in a Jewish body. But, as Bastide observes, "this Jewish body was not white enough for them." [19] As a result, "the dark hair that Christ was thought to have had came to be rendered as very light-colored, and his big dark eyes as blue." [20] The bleaching process in which Christ's hair and beard assumed the color of sunshine, symbolizing the brightness of the light above, and his eyes, the color of the sky from which he descended and to which he returned marked the entire history of Western painting. Bastide rightly notes that "the progressive Aryanization of Christ is in strict accordance with the logic of the color symbolism," namely, that "it was necessary that this man, the incarnation of God, be as far removed as possible from everything that could suggest darkness or blackness, even indirectly." [21]

Not only the person of Jesus was whitened but also his garments to indicate his divinity. And all those closely associated with Christ underwent a whitening process. Thus the Semitic mother of Christ was depicted as a blond woman and her garments too were either white or blue signifying the heavenly. Just as white symbolized the chastity and virginity of Christ, so it was with Mary, his mother. In honoring Mary, everything connected with her service was white. Thus, "Her altars are white, the ornaments of the priests officiating are white, and white is worn on her festival day. This meaning is also present in the use of white garments for young girls, for the bride." [22]

After the Mother of Jesus comes the Pope of Rome who is called the Vicar of Christ, the visible representative of God upon earth. He too as being closely associated with Christ wears white garments as symbolic of divinity and grace.[23]

The color symbolism of white as superior to black is illustrated in the paintings of The Three Kings or the Three Wise Men (Magi) who came to worship Christ, the newborn child. They were first depicted as white men, and later as representatives of the three great continents: Europe, Asia, and Africa. What is interesting in the paintings is that Balthasar, the Negro King, was situated behind the other two Magi, or even sometimes kneeling closest to the Babe, but never between the other two.[24] Furthermore, he is represented as giving to the fair-haired child amidst the golden straw, the gift of myrrh, a yellowish-brown to reddish-brown aromatic gum resin with a bitter slightly pungent taste while the other two gave gold and frankincense. Commenting on the painting of the Magi, Bastide observes that "racism subsisted in the disguised form of a patronizing attitude in this first attempt to remove the demoniac symbolism from the black skin." [25]

The Christian saints, too, had to be symbolized by white. As Evarts notes, "White, because it is pure and untouched, becomes also the symbol of chastity, and is used with this meaning in the early Christian paintings as the background of the saints." [26] The result of this whitening process is that black saints were either ignored, whitened, or depicted as second class saints. Thus, "St. Mauritius, a commander of the Roman legions in Egypt who was martyred there, was originally depicted as white but then as a Moor, and finally in the thirteenth century as a Negro." [27] Again, because of the association of the color black with sin and the demoniacal, the Church long ignored the black saint, Benedict of Palermo, known as St. Benedict the Moor, but finally officialized him only because of the need to develop the missions in Africa and to furnish the slaves in the Western Hemisphere with a model to follow.

The mystic symbolism in which white stands for sanctity, grace, and black, for sin, damnation, which the Church tried to break by officially recognizing Benedict the Moor as a saint of the Church, returns in another form. The mystical symbolism is converted to the aesthetic. Moral evil now takes the form of ugliness. Thus, St. Benedict, in order to escape temptations relating to the other sex, prayed to God to make him ugly, so God turned his skin black.[28] This shift does not mean that the symbolism at the level of the mystical no longer holds. No, white is still the symbol for supreme sanctity. The Virgin Mary and Christ stayed white; the colored saints—e.g., St. Mauritius, St. Benedict the Moor, St. Iphigenia the Mulatto, and St. Balthasar the Negro King—are only intermediaries. Because they remain well below Christ and Mary, the mystical symbolism remains intact. Instead of showing the unity of different races, the inclusion of black saints in the comunity of saints rather symbolizes the differences, the abyss between races, the stratification in a multiracial society.[29] The only difference in the symbolism is that instead of polar opposites, black and white now are arranged in a hierarchy in which the color black is subordinate. Thus, racism takes another form.

To counteract this new form of racism as a subordination of black peoples to the whites, Indian serfs and African slaves and mulattos prayed to white saints to show that they belonged to the race of the masters. Bastide relates a folk rumor according to which a mulatto in Brazil "would put the portrait of his Negro mother in the kitchen and that of his white father in the parlor. He would shun colored saints and invoke only the aid of white saints, even though these were claimed by pure white people to belong exclusively to them." [30] Bastide further notes interestingly that "the mulattos invented the brotherhood of the Cord of St. Francis in order to enter, by the back door so to speak, the aristocratic church of the Franciscans and to mingle with the white people there." [31]

The theology of sex and marriage has its roots too in color symbolism. As early as the sixteenth century, English perception integrated sexuality with blackness, a perception imbedded deep in Elizabethan culture.[32] According to an English adventurer by the name of George Best, the source of Negro blackness is due to a carnal or sexual sin as narrated in scripture:

> Noah "commanded" his sons and their wives to behold God "with reverence and feare," and that "while they remained in the Arke, they should use continencie, and abstaine from carnall copulation with their wives: . . . which good instructions and exhortations notwithstanding his wicked sonne Cham disobeyed, and being perswaded that the first childe borne after the flood . . . should inherite . . . all the dominions of the arth, hee . . . used company with his wife, and craftily went about thereby to dis-inherit the off-spring of his other two brethren." To punish this "wicked and detestable fact," God willed that "a sonne should bee born whose name was Chus, who not onely it selfe, but all his posteritie after him should bee so blacke and lothsome, that it might remain a spectacle of disobedience to all the worlde. And of this blacke and cursed Chus came all these blacke Moores which are in Africa." [33]

Thus, Best linked "disobedience" with "carnall copulation" with something "black and lothsome." The implication running throughout this extraordinary exegesis, notes Jordan, is that God had originally created man not only "Angelike" but "white." [34] Let us follow the implications of the connection between a black skin and sexual sin in the attitude toward sex and marriage.

Thus, sin is associated with the sexual, the carnal or emotional, the passions; while grace and sanctity have to do with the virginal, the pure. The color symbolism of black as evil, sinful, and white as pure, virginal is transposed to the realm of sex and marriage. Bastide notes that in South America, "a distinction is always made between a white woman, the object of legitimate courtship and marriage who is worshipped like the Holy Virgin, and the colored woman, the mistress who is an object of pleasure." [35] The colored woman symbolizes carnal pleasure, sin. This symbolism was at the base of Baudelaire's desire when he "actually sought in his colored sweetheart the sensation of sin through carnal love with a woman whose color suggested the flames of Hades." [36] The South American may not fully realize as did Baudelaire the working of this symbolism, but it nevertheless operates.[37] For him too, "a woman of color is considered to be a person of sheer voluptuousness. The slightest gesture she makes, such as the balanced sway of her body as she walks barefoot, is looked upon as a call of the female sex to the male. On the other hand, the white woman is desexualized, if not disincarnated or at least dematerialized." [38]

In marriage the symbolism too is operative. Thus, "a too carnal enjoyment of the wife would have taken on the aspect of a kind of incest, degrading to both the white man and the white woman. White signified purity, innocence and virginity. A woman whose skin was not entirely white suggested the carnal merely by her color. She became, therefore, the legitimate object of enjoyment." [39]

The color symbolism applied to sex and marriage found in Catholic consciousness is also operative in Protestant thought.

As Bastide observes, "the Protestant's association of the color black with the devil and sin was as strong as the Catholic's. But the Protestant, feeling sure that his soul would go straight to hell, placed the bulwark of Puritanism between himself and the temptation of the woman with color-tinted skin." [40]

Puritanism helped the white man from succumbing to the carnal allurement of the colored woman by arousing fear in him through the suggestion that the contagiousness of color was associated with the contagiousness of sin. He was made to believe that the mere presence of a dark-skinned woman sullied his eyes and marked his flesh. He was taught that the power of the Devil was such that contact with African women who bore the color of the Prince of Darkness would be contact with the Devil. Besides these moral barriers, aesthetic ones were also put up. Thus, a black skin was associated with ugliness, with stain and pollution, with unbearable odors and with oiliness. When these moral and aesthetic barriers proved ineffective, legal barriers were established, namely, segregation by color in public places: in churches, in eating places, in trains and streetcars, in theaters, and in schools, so white children could not be influenced by the Devil working through colored children.[41]

The Protestant negative position on miscegenation while justified on the surface by rationalizations about the ill effects of mixed marriages was really based at bottom on the hidden symbolism of sin being a stain and a pollution which blackened the white person.[42]

Thus, over and above any historical and economic factors, the causes of segregation are to be found in the religious ideas of white being a symbol of purity and black a symbol of sin. For Catholics, the white woman was a symbol of the Madonna, hence like her, she was elevated to almost inaccessible rank. For the Protestants, the black woman was a source of sin due to the contagiousness of sin through color, hence, spiritual hygiene was inculcated by the practice of strict family morals and a stern Puritanism.[43]

The powerful pressures on behavior exerted by the symbolisms just discussed affect not only whites but blacks as well. Thus, blacks conditioned by Western culture behave toward white and black women according to the Western color symbolism. This, of course, produces a dilemma for the black man which Eldridge Cleaver notes. Thus one of the characters in his book says: [44]

> But I'm stuck with myself and I accept my own thought about things. For instance, I don't know just how it works, I mean I can't analyze it, but I know that white man made the black woman the symbol of slavery and the white woman the symbol of freedom. Every time I embrace a black woman I'm embracing slavery, and when I put my arms around a white woman, well, I'm hugging freedom.[44]

The root of the symbolism from the theological point of view is the color white as symbolic of grace and virtue, and black as symbolic of the slavery of sin and Satan.

The allegory continues: "The white man forbade me to have the white woman on pain of death. Literally, if I touched a white woman it would cost me my life. Men die for freedom, but black men die for white women, who are the symbol of freedom." [45] Again, the religious root of the white woman being taboo to the black man is the elevation of the white woman on a pedestal, inaccessible like the Blessed Virgin. This insight is expressed by the character Lazarus in the allegory: "He who worships the Virgin Mary will lust for the beautiful dumb blonde." [46] The same idea is expressed by another character in the allegory (the Accused):

"The white woman is more than a woman to me. She's like a goddess, a symbol. My love for her is religious and beyond fulfillment. I worship her. I love a white woman's dirty drawers." [47] The Accused in his self-reflection thinks that his attitude toward the white woman has been inherited from his father and from his father's father and as far back as one can go into slavery. He notes that his desire for the white woman is like a cancer devouring his brain and eating his heart out. But beyond attributing the source of this attitude to his ancestors, he cannot find the answer.[48]

Let us move on to an examination of the symbolism of color in Calvinism as applied to other areas besides that of sex and marriage. We already noted that whiteness stood for grace, blackness for sin and damnation. Grace is a sign of election, that is, a sign of God's favor which predestines one to heaven. The possession of the knowledge of God gave light to one's mind, driving away the darkness. This knowledge is a grace from God. Christians insofar as they are gifted with the knowledge of God are the elect. In comparison to them, non-Christians dwelt in darkness. When the Calvinists came to the New World and found there the Indians they tried to convert them to the Faith. But the Indians preferred their own practices and gods to the laws of the Christian God. This, to the Calvinists, was a sign of negative predestination; for persevering in diabolical practices, God refused to give his grace to them. As Bastide notes, "the association of the darker color of the skin with a parallel blackness of the soul became for the Puritans arriving in the New World a fact of experience. The symbolism of color was confirmed as an obvious truth." [49]

On the other hand, the small band of Calvinists who observed the laws of God and were Christians in the fullest sense of the term were the chosen people of God. And just as in the Old Testament the chosen people of God (the

Qahal Yahweh) were given the Holy Land flowing with milk and honey, so they were given the New World as God's own country. According to their founder in his *Commentary on Matthew*, the Calvinists were God's chosen flock whom he esteems more than all the rest of the world.[50] Thus, the black-white color symbolism took the form of election, on the one hand, and damnation or reprobation, on the other. On God's right hand are the sheep, on his left, the goats. The Calvinists as the pioneering band saw themselves as the elect, the small flock (*pusillus grex*) of God, and the Indians as the reprobates, dwelling in sin and darkness of ignorance from which the elect of God must guard themselves as from a contagious disease.

The same ideas noted above motivated the small band of Calvinists in South Africa. These ideas were institutionalized in the form of *apartheid*.[51] As Bastide notes, "The white community feels itself to be a community elected by God to make fertile a land that the non-Europeans could not exploit. The natives have cast themselves away from divine election because they have not used properly the talents God has given them." [52] Thus, dark skin came to symbolize both in Africa and in America superstition, magic, diabolical powers —in short, ignorance of the saving truth of the Gospel, due to stubbornness of will. It signified blackness of soul in comparison to the white person's soul and the whiteness of his spirit.

The Catholic missionaries' attitude toward the dark-skinned peoples in the colonial countries was not much different from that of the Calvinists since they proceed from a common color symbolism. Thus for the Catholic missionaries, Christians (Westerners) had the light of faith, the dark-skinned pagans had only their reasons ignorant of revelation. Hence the natives dwelt in darkness under the sway of diabolical spirits. The association of a black skin with ignorance, darkness of mind, and diabolical spirits was expressed by Francisco Pigafetta, who, in talking about his travels with Ferdinand Magellan likened the "black people" of Brazil to "enemies of Hell." [53]

It is not necessary to go further into an examination of how Western color symbolism influenced religious behavior and practice. For the purposes of our study the evidence presented here is, I hope, sufficient.[54]

3

WESTERN COLOR SYMBOLISM SECULARIZED

I n this chapter we will study the use made of the religious color symbolism of black and white in secular literature and in the economic realm.

Let us first discuss the influence of the religious symbolism on literature. According to Don Cameron Allen, the symbolic interpretation of color from the Church ritual and religious art of the Middle Ages became an intrinsic form of symbolism in the English literature of the sixteenth century in a form more widespread than it had been in medieval times.[1] "The color black," says Allen, "is used universally in the sixteenth century to signify as it does today sorrow and mourning." [2] By way of contrast, "the color white is quite naturally used as a symbol of innocence and virginity." [3] Harold Isaacs also notes that "the carry-over of the Bible's imagery into the common usage, visible in Chaucer and Milton, is richly illustrated in Shakespeare, whose impact on the English language has hardly been less great than that of the Bible itself." [4] Thus, in *Love's Labour's Lost,* the king who chides Biron for loving an "Ethiope," namely, Rosaline, who is called "black as ebony" says:

Black is the badge of hell,
The hue of the dungeon and the suit of night.[5]

Caroline F. E. Spurgeon also finds "the general light and darkness symbolism reinforced by touches of both black and white" in *Romeo and Juliet*.[6] Thus Rosaline in Romeo's eyes compared to Juliet is but a crow while Juliet is a snowy dove, and Juliet in her turn declares that Romeo will

. . . lie upon the wings of night
Whiter than new snow on a raven's back.[7]

But it is in *Othello* that the symbolism of black and white is expressed throughout.[8] There is a symbolic joining of sin, the devil, sex with blackness of skin and beauty, purity, innocence with whiteness. The contrasting symbolism is summed up in Iago's contemptuous use of "black ram" and "white ewe" (Oth. 1.1.88). Desdemona's white skin symbolizes purity, fairness, innocence:

Nor scar that whiter skin of hers than snow
And smooth as monumental alabaster (5.2.4).

Blackness symbolizes sexuality as when Iago tells the agitated Brabantino that "an old black ram is tupping your white ewe." "This was not merely the language of (as we say) a 'dirty' mind; it was the integrated imagery of blackness and whiteness," according to Jordan.[9]

Blackness as sin is implied in Othello's agonized cry upon suspecting Desdemona of infidelity:

Her name, that was as fresh
As Dian's visage, is now begrimed and black
As mine own face (3.3.386)

Western Color Symbolism Secularized   *43*

Blackness symbolizes the devil, and white, the angelic, as when Othello groans to Emilia, " 'Twas I that killed her," and Emilia responds:

> O! the more angel she
> And you the blacker devil

P. J. Heather studies the color symbolism of black and white from Chaucer to Shakespeare, Milton, Shelley and Tennyson. In Shakespeare he summarizes the uses of the term black: [10]

> death's black veil; black as death, black as ink; black as a crow; and, let the devil wear black; damn'd as black; the devil damn thee black; a black deed; black villainy; black sins.

In Milton black is used "in connection with hell, death and sin; sorrow; drugs; adverse to life; he also wrote of black humours, black Perdition, and mentions black as the hue of Wisdom." Shelley uses black in connection with death, despair, suggestions, parricide, guilty world, vice, name, and demon forms. And in Tennyson, black is used in connection with lies, blood, the devil and fiend.

Heather next studies the symbolism of white in the above-mentioned writers [11] and finds it applied in numerous instances with positive signification and only in rare occasions does it have a negative significance. White is applied in a positive sense by Shakespeare to convey sanctity, virtue, innocence and peace but is also used in connection with death. Tennyson also applies white to the robe of saints, life, truth, a white lie, blamelessness, innocence, maidens in white, knights in white, virginity, maiden's hand, the black sheep made white and only as an exception is it applied to the whiteness of death and of sin. Milton applies white to vestments, to maidens in white. Shelley follows Shakespeare and Tennyson in speaking of the whiteness of death but differs from them in that to him death at times appeared to be black. But on the whole, whiteness for Shelley has a positive signification as in the whiteness of innocence and the whiteness of truth. Whiteness and blackness are also used in connection with superhuman powers and spirits. Thus Shakespeare, Shelley, and Tennyson refer to angel whiteness, angels robed in white and white as angels, which use is constrasted to the use of black in black enchantment, black magicians, black fairies, black hags.

Studies in the symbolism of Hawthorne, Poe and Melville also show the major tendency to use white as a symbol of various forms of goodness and black as the symbol of evil.[12] The same symbolism appears in stories written for children. Thus, Harold Isaac mentions the Dr. Dolittle stories avidly read by both European and American children since 1920.[13] In this book, Dr. Dolittle, an animal doctor, travels to Africa to cure monkeys of a plague. While in Africa he and his entourage of animal helpers become prisoners of a black king who has a son, Prince Bumpo, an ugly gnome-like black man with a huge nose that covers most of his face. The Prince has a yearning to become a *white* prince, since he was rejected by The Sleeping Beauty who, upon being awakened by the kiss of Prince Bumpo, cried out "Oh, he's black!" and she ran away and wouldn't marry him. The Prince therefore asks Dr. Dolittle to turn him white—not just with blond hair but with blue eyes too. The doctor concocts a paste which whitens Bumpo's face only long enough for the doctor and his entourage to escape. In the morning Bumpo wakes up as black as ever. The duck in the doctor's entourage makes the final comment: "Serve him right if he does turn black again. I hope it is a dark black."

Children today see the same black-white symbolism in the movies and on television programs that are made by Hollywood. For example, in westerns, the cowboy-hero always wears a white hat and rides a white horse while the cowboy villain always a black hat and a black horse.[14] And, as we noted earlier, the everyday language of the common man is shot through with the same symbolism.[15] But this very brief and cursory survey of literature is sufficient to show the transference of the religious symbolism imbedded in Western theology and religious practice into secular writing. Our next task is to show how the same religious symbolism transferred to the cultural level is now pressed into the service of economic exploitation.

To see the transference of the black-white symbolism from the theological to the economic, the key concept is that of election. In the theological sense, white skin came to mean the possession of grace and spiritual riches; black skin, on the other hand, meant spiritual poverty, the "voluntary and stubborn abandonment of a race in sin." [16]

Under the influence of Calvinism and later Puritanism, however, the notion of election became secularized to mean economic and material success. The whiteness or blackness of the skin accordingly came to have a secular meaning also. Thus whiteness of skin came to symbolize material, scientific and technological successes while blackness of skin came to be equated with a prescientific mentality, with economic poverty and with ignorance. As Bastide notes: [17]

The community of the whites had no sense of loss when it came to consider itself as the small flock of the select. Its economic success was proof of divine grace, just as the situation of the blacks was the sign of their rejection.

Thus, the economic success of the white Europeans is considered by them as a sure sign and confirmation of their divine election. God himself has chosen the white peoples to be the elect just as of old Yahweh called the Hebrews to be his chosen people.

Max Weber has analyzed more fully how Calvinistic and English Puritan theologies came to give a theological basis and sanction for the success of capitalism in the West.[18] Weber notes that Calvinism shared with Catholicism and Lutheranism the view that only a small portion of men are chosen for eternal grace. But the notion of predestination was given a peculiar twist by Calvinism. The common problem for all Christian sects is how the believer knows that he is in God's favor, that he is one of the elect. Now for Calvinism, all magical means of knowing God's will and favor are to be eliminated.[19] The conceptualist trend which repudiated all magical means to salvation as superstition and sin and which was helped along in this direction by Hellenistic scientific thought found its logical conclusion in Calvinism and Puritanism.[20] Thus, "the genuine Puritan even rejected all signs of religious ceremony at the grave and buried his nearest and dearest without song or ritual in order that no superstition, no trust in the effects of magical and sacramental forces on salvation, should creep in." [21]

How then is the Calvinist believer to identify true faith and arrive at *certitudo salutis* (certainty of salvation)? It was by a type of Christian conduct which served to increase the glory of God. This type of Christian conduct, as is noted in 2 Cor. 13:5, was through good works. But good works were not a means of attaining salvation; rather, they were the indispensable sign of election. "They are the technical means, not of purchasing salvation, but of getting rid of the fear of damnation. In this sense they are occasionally referred to as directly necessary for salvation or the *possessio salutis* is made conditional on them." [22]

What was meant by good works? Here Calvinism gave a new emphasis to the word. For it did not mean so much "religious" good works such as frequenting the sacraments for this would mean a reversal to magic in which the priest as magician performs the miracle of transubstantiation as worldly activity. The result was an ethic founded on the doctrine of predestination except that instead of the spiritual aristocracy of monks we then find the spiritual aristocracy of the predestined saints of God within the world. Thus, Puritan morality as "a methodically rationalized ethical conduct," slammed the door of the monastery behind it and strode into the marketplace of life.[23]

For Weber, worldly activity in the world was for the Puritan the meaning of the divine calling, not, "as with Luther, on the acceptance of the lot which God has irretrievably assigned to man." But the question now for the believer was the measure by which one can gauge the usefulness of the calling. In practice "the most important criterion is found in private profitableness." [24] In the writings of Puritan Divines (*Works of the Puritan Divines,* London, 1845-8), Weber notes the following advice: [25]

If that God, whose hand the Puritan sees in all the occurrencies of life, shows one of His elect a chance of profit, he must do it with a purpose. Hence the faithful Christian must follow the call by taking advantage of the opportunity. 'If God show you a way in which you may lawfully get more than in another way (without wrong to your soul or to any other), if you refuse this, and choose the less gainful way, you cross one of the ends of your calling, and you refuse to be God's steward, and to accept His gifts and use them for Him when He requireth it: you may labour to be rich for God, though not for the flesh and sin.'

Thus, the providential interpretation of profit-making justifying the activities of the business man was partly based on the scriptural parable of the servant who was rejected because he did not increase the talents which were entrusted to him.[26]

From the point of view of color symbolism, the rejected servant represented blacks who by not having progressed economically, did not increase the talents entrusted to them and therefore were rejected. The whites, on the other hand, have progressed economically, hence they represent the good servant who increased the talents entrusted to him and was therefore rewarded entrance into the kingdom of the master. Thus, the Puritan ethic contained within it the color symbolism of black and white, black as a sign of rejection and white as a sign of election. This symbolism transferred to skin color meant the election of white peoples and the rejection of black peoples, except that the sign of election is now the secular notion of economic wealth rather than the supernatural reality of grace.

We might speculate here and ask whether the nonassociation of whites with blacks at the economic level and the resultant economic stagnation of blacks may not be partly due to the transference of the theological symbolism of black as sinful to the economic level. Thus, just as the reason for the ban on racial intermarriage in the past was partly due to the fear of contamination by sin—in this case, black skin being a symbol of sin—so, the reason for assigning blacks to be "hewers of wood and drawers of water" is the religious belief that blacks symbolized sin—in this case, economic poverty.

While whites saw the successful struggle from poverty as a sign of God's favor on them, they felt no corresponding need on the part of blacks to better their economic lot for they were predestined to be in that state, nor did the whites attempt to help blacks economically for one does not do commerce with sin which would contaminate one. Whether

that the only expense; he has really spent, or rather thrown away, five shillings besides.

Remember, that credit is money. If a man lets his money lie in my hands after it is due, he gives me the interest, or so much as I can make of it during that time. This amounts to a considerable sum where a man has good and large credit, and makes good use of it.

Remember, that money is of the prolific, generating nature. Money can beget money, and its offspring can beget more, and so on. Five shillings turned is six, turned again it is seven and threepence, and so on, till it becomes a hundred pounds. The more there is of it, the more it produces every turning, so that the profits rise quicker and quicker. He that kills a breeding-sow, destroys all her offspring to the thousandth generation. He that murders a crown, destroys all that it might have produced, even scores of pounds.

Much of the Puritan ethic survives in utilitarianism. Notice in the above passage the inculcation of the Puritan virtues of honesty, punctuality, frugality, the only difference being that these are now preached as natural virtues instead of super- natural ones.

The Puritan notion of election based on the scriptural parable of the good servant who was numbered among the elect because he used his talents to the utmost is implicit in the passage. In fact, as Max Weber observes, the Calvinist father of Benjamin Franklin drummed into his son the quo- tation from the Bible, "Seest thou a man diligent in his busi- ness? He shall stand before kings" (Prov. 22:29).[30] Thus much of Franklin's early Calvinistic training survives in his ethics which is a fusion of Puritan and utilitarian ethics. For Franklin, "the earning of money within the modern eco- nomic order is, so long as it is done legally, the result and the expression of virtue and proficiency in a calling." [31] This ethics of Franklin was preached however to white slave owners and other businessmen. The utilitarian principle of the greatest good or happiness for the greatest number did not apply to black slaves who were not considered citizens let alone human beings. Utilitarian economics was bourgeois economics, hence, here again the conflict between light and darkness and the election of white over black survive.

The bourgeois economics of pre-civil war America was the result of a fusion of Calvinism and utilitarianism.[32] But in the post-civil war period, the influence of Jefferson and Franklin faded and the influence of Herbert Spencer gradually assumed prominence.[33] This new influence resulted in a new notion of election which is implicit in the consciousness of what William Marnell calls the American Philistine and whom he describes as follows: [34]

> The American Philistine, however, achieved his full development at a date late enough for a further fusion to take place in him, a fusion of social Darwinism with everything else that went into his ideological composition. As a utilitarian whose explicit utilitarianism is by now rather submerged by everything piled on top of it, he will continue to believe in the greatest happiness of the greatest number as the proper objective of the social order. As an American he will believe that the greatest happiness will be achieved by the greatest number when they pursue happiness, along with life and liberty, after the philosophy enunciated in the Declaration of Independence. As inheritor of the Calvinist tradition, aided by his conviction that Calvinism included among its tenets the manifest favor of the Almighty to His elect upon earth, he will believe that his success in achieving

material wealth and the happiness that goes with it will give witness to the fact that he is one of the anointed. As a believer in social Darwinism he will believe that the laissez faire to which he subscribes as a utilitarian is part of an inexorable and unalterable law of nature leading mankind onward and upward on the evolutionary principle, but leading individuals onward and upward at varying speeds and to varying heights which are determined by their individual abilities.

Thus, the Darwinian theory of evolution supported the age of enterprise: "In nature, the fittest rise to positions of dominance, the less fit are eliminated. Thus the species slowly improves through natural selection, so long as no extraneous influence interferes." In terms of this theory, " 'Fitness' was defined in terms of material success, because nature is incapable of recognizing another standard. The elite, the saints of the new religion, therefore, were those who had proved their native superiority by their survival value. This will be recognized as the Puritan idea of 'election' in modern dress; the supporting rationale was different, but the implications were almost indistinguishable." [35]

The full pattern of American Philistinism is revealed in William Graham Sumner, professor of political and social science at Yale University from 1872 until his death in 1910. His influence was mainly responsible for the rise of the Fisks, Goulds, Morgans, Carnegies and Rockefellers. As Marnell observes, the "key to his concept lies in his fundamentally simple and in a curious way Calvinistic sort of materialism. God's anointed are the prosperous. The sound social order is the fiscally sound social order. Every stage in the development of civilization has been made possible by capital. Hence it is the capitalist who carries the torch of civilization.

Treasure will not rust nor will moth corrupt it if it is invested in productive enterprise. Not the truth but the savings accounts shall make you free." [36] As Sumner himself says: [37]

> It may be said, then, that liberty is to be found at the summit of civilization, and that those who have the resources of civilization at their command are the only ones who are free. But the resources of civilization are capital; and so it follows that the capitalists are free, or, to avoid ambiguities in the word capitalist, that the rich are free. Popular language, which speaks of the rich as independent, has long carried an affirmation upon this point. In reality the thirst for wealth is a thirst for this independence of the ills of life, and the interdependence of wealth on civilization and civilization on wealth is the reason why the science of wealth is concerned with the prime conditions of human welfare, and why all denunciations of desire to increase or to win wealth are worse than childish.

Applying the ideas of Spencer and Sumner, we hear John D. Rockefeller saying to a Sunday-school class: "The growth of a large business is merely the survival of the fittest. . . . The American Beauty rose can be produced in the splendor and fragrance which bring cheer to its beholder only by sacrificing the early buds which grow up around it." [38] And as with the rose so with Standard Oil: "This is not an evil tendency in business. It is merely the working-out of a law of nature and a law of God." [39] Andrew Carnegie had similar convictions after reading Darwin and Spencer: "I remember that light came as in a flood and all was clear . . . not only had I got rid of theology and the supernatural, but I had found the truth of evolution. 'All is well since all grows better,' became my motto, my true source of comfort." [40]

The Depression, however, dealt the death blow to social Darwinism which is based on the premise that "all works for the best when things are left alone, that the course of human progress is as inexorable as it is inspiring." [41] Things could not be left alone to take their course. Something had to be done by government: the Agricultural Adjustment Act, the National Industrial Recovery Act with its codes of fair competition designed to bring health back to the body economic; the Civilian Conservation Corps Act, the TVA, etc. These actions of the government proved very successful. Thus the influence of pragmatism began. For pragmatism, truth is successful experience as determined by experiment; it is something that develops. As Marnell observes, "The New Dealers thought of the Constitution as an instrument and not a charter. . . . The entire course of the New Deal was an application to American life, in the course of the worst internal crisis in all American history except the Civil War, of the philosophy of pragmatism." [42]

The pragmatist philosophy or rather method of applying the scientific method of experiment to life gave rise to an elite group, the scientific and managerial class. Again, the notion of election symbolized by the superiority of white over black survives. In America the white Anglo-Saxon Protestants are the top scientists and hold the highest positions of authority and possess most of the wealth of the country. And before the world, white America is the elect because of its dominance in science and technology and its superior ability in business management and systems analysis.

From our brief and very cursory survey of the Western ethic of election, we see that the notion evolved as cultural norms evolved. Thus, in the age of belief (the Middle Ages), the possession of Christianity as the true light was the sign of election, and this meant the Christian West; in the age of reason, the sign of election was the possession of reason manifested in the presence of developed philosophies which again were found only in the West. In the age of science and technology, success in the economic and scientific realms was a sign of election and again we find this success verified in the West.

Today, because of the wondrous success of capitalism and the rational spirit of science, it is not deemed necessary to maintain the Western symbolism of color by religious and supernatural means. As Bastide observes, to the white man the "materialistic approach of the capitalistic economy and also the rational spirit of science became the new religion." [43] But even in the "new religion" the religious color symbolism of light and darkness, white and black, remains. As Bastide rightly observes: [44]

Association with the devil and sin have no place in the concept of the universe introduced in the late-nineteenth century. But the "frontier complex" between two conflicting mentalities has held firm. Black and white have taken on other meanings: These meanings still follow, however, the basic antithesis founded centuries before on the white purity of the elect and the blackness of Satan. Because this symbolism became secularized, it survived the collapse of the old Christian code of ethics and the advent of another system of ideas. The Christian tree had been uprooted, but had left root fragments that continued to creep obscurely under the surface.

4

PSYCHOLOGICAL EFFECTS OF WESTERN COLOR SYMBOLISM

We would like to discuss here the psychological effects of Western color symbolism on both blacks and whites.

From the psychoanalytic point of view, darkness or blackness is the symbol of the unconscious; whiteness or light of the conscious. Western color symbolism in psychoanalytic terms is precisely the expression at the conscious level of the flight from the unconscious.[1] When the negative attitude toward the unconscious symbolized as darkness is transferred to peoples with dark skin color, it results in racism. Racism in psychoanalytic terms is a denial of the unconscious.

Before we analyze more fully the relation between the Western symbolism of color and the unconscious, let us first consider the psychological effects of the color symbolism at the conscious level. Let me quote the following poem widely read by children in the past and see how it affected psychologically those who read it: [2]

My mother bore me in the southern wild,
And I am black, but O! my soul is white;

White as an angel is the English child,
But I am black, as if bereav'd of light.

My mother . . . began to say:

. . . And we are put on earth a little space
That we may learn to bear the beams of love;
And these black bodies and this sunburnt face
Is but a cloud, and like a shady grove.

For when our souls have learn'd the heat to bear,
The cloud will vanish; we shall hear His voice,
Saying: "Come out from the grove, My love and care,
And round My golden tent like lambs rejoice."

Thus did my mother say, and kissed me;
And thus I say to little English boy.
When I from black and he from white cloud free,
And round the tent of God like lambs we joy,

I'll shade him from the heat, till he can bear
To lean in joy upon our Father's knee;
And then I'll stand and stroke his silver hair,
And be like him, and he will then love me.

Now a white child reading the poem has his self-esteem
enhanced and confirmed while a black child derives a negative self-image from the poem. The black child must flee
darkness and become white—in soul, character, and skin
—to be loved. This in effect is to flee from himself. Thus,
at an early age a psychological crisis of identity is induced
in him. But this is also true for the white child in whom an
inflated ego is nurtured.

Let us give an example from children's stories. This one is
about "The Story of Two Little Lambs." [3]

A little white lamb strays from the flock and is lost and meets a little black lamb in the forest. Says the little black lamb: "You are what they call a White Lamb, and White Lambs have a good home and good things all the time, and they say that they have a good Shepherd; but I am only a black one . . . some day when we meet the good Shepherd (if we ever do chance to meet Him) He will take us too, and bring us to the White Lambs' fold.

To this the white lamb replies: "I don't think He would like you very much for I have always been told that He wants His Sheep and Lambs to have very white, white wool and you are black." The Shepherd Jesus comes to recover his stray white lamb and promises that he can wash him clean and white again, and is about to leave when the little black lamb speaks up and says he wishes he was one of Jesus' lambs too. "But it's no use," he says, "for they say you only want White Sheep and Lambs and cannot bear black wool, so I cannot be the sort of Lamb you want." To which Jesus replies: "Did you not hear that I can wash away the stains and make my little Lamb white again?" "But, good Shepherd," interposes the little white lamb, "that Lamb has always been black. . . . It isn't your Lamb, it's quite another sort." Jesus is sad and angry. "Who said the Black Lambs were not mine? Who said I do not want them?"

So he takes up both little lambs, carries them to a stream in which he washes them, "and when they came out they were both white, as white as snow. They bleated for joy and jumped around the Shepherd, and then they laid their little heads in His tender hand, and He stroked them lovingly.

Again, in the story, the white child gets a psychological boost, while the black child gets only a psychological sense of inferiority. It is not these particular examples that are important but the accumulated psychological effect produced by such examples and countless others to which the child is exposed such as comic books, pictures, television shows, and the very language itself of the culture, its institutions and mores, all of them cumulatively imposing a color symbolism in which white is good and black evil. The psychological effects induced by this color symbolism do not stay merely at the level of the ego but affect the unconscious.

In Freudian terms, the realm of the unconscious is established when the individual or a group refuses to admit in its conscious life an idea, purpose or desire. This rejection by the group or individual of a purpose or idea which is nevertheless his is repression.[4]

Repression takes two forms: the repression of self and aggression toward others. Now the idea of blackness or darkness is a negative one in Western thought. The effect is to repress this idea, hence to keep it out of consciousness. It is making the idea invisible. In relation to aggression as the effect of repression, white society logically enough has sought to render black invisible or at least inferior. Ralph Ellison has taken note of this mode of aggression by the very title of his book, *The Invisible Man*.[5] But let us first consider the effect of repression in the psyche of Western man himself.

Frantz Fanon, a Negro and a psychiatrist, using the framework of Jungian psychology, finds European civilization as characterized by the presence at the heart of the collective unconscious of an archetype: "An expression of the bad instincts, of the darkness inherent in every ego, of the civilized savage, the Negro who slumbers in every white man."[6] Whatever be one's understanding of the collective unconscious[7] its presence is however unquestioned. Following Fanon's view that the collective unconscious is the unreflected imposition of a culture rather than the hereditary cerebral structure, Fanon then describes the symbols found in the remotest depth of the European unconscious, which is a black hollow. In this black hollow we find the black man as the symbol of Evil. Says Fanon, "The archetype of the lowest values is represented by the Negro." He elaborates on this in a lengthy passage worth quoting: [8]

> *In Europe, the black man is the symbol of Evil* (italics Fanon) . . . The torturer is the black man, Satan is black, one talks of shadows, when one is dirty one is black— whether one is thinking of physical dirtiness or of moral dirtiness. It would be astonishing, if the trouble were taken to bring them all together, to see the vast number of expressions that make the black man the equivalent of sin. In Europe, whether concretely or symbolically, the black man stands for the bad side of the character. As long as one cannot understand this fact, one is doomed to talk in circles about the 'black problem'. Blackness, darkness, shadow, shades, night, the labyrinths of the earth, abysmal depths, blacken someone's reputation; and, on the other side, the bright look of innocence, the white dove of peace, magical, heavenly light. A magnificent blond child—how much peace there is in that phrase, how much joy, and above all how much hope! There is no comparison with a magnificent black child: literally, such a thing is unwonted. Just the same, I shall not go back into the stories of black angels. In Europe, that is to say, in every civilized and civilizing country, the Negro is the symbol of sin.

Another psychologist, Joel Kovel, also notes a similar psychic organization at the level of the unconscious in which black "represents the shade of evil, the devil's aspect, night, separation, loneliness, sin, dirt, excrement, the inside of the body; and white represents the mark of good, the token of innocence, purity, cleanliness, spirituality, virtue, hope." [9]

Kovel observes rightly that the imposition of an extreme polarity upon the world in which white is all good and black all bad results in the diminishment not only of the object to which the value of black is projected but also of the perpetrator upon whom the value of white is imposed.[10]

The result of the color symbolism on the perpetrator of it is noted by Kovel. Thus he says that "by oppressing and blackening the dark-skinned races, Caucasians pursue a course that whitens their own self, making it chalky, abstract, separated—eventually blank and invisible. And invisibility is no mere frustration, nor even simply a loss; it becomes for the white man a white cold flame that endlessly dissolves all before it. Invisibility—which was imposed on blacks but sprang from whites—is the full horror; and, in our times, the ground for totalitarianism." [11]

Using the novel of Melville, *Moby Dick,* which anticipates Freud's category of the unconscious, Kovel also observes that "whiteness brings power and horror alike, the two feeding upon each other across the splitting of the historical ego. Splitting, denial, negation of darkness create within an emptiness which makes the world a pasteboard mask, deadened and suitable to be worked over." [12] And the technology and consumerism which are the symbols of white power have resulted in the acquisition of lifeless, pleasureless, and abstracted matter and the extension of the market principle to the entire universe has produced destruction and death, pollution, waste, and the icy grip of white death.[13] Thus the extreme polarity of the black-white symbolism has resulted in whiteness ironically standing for blankness, the attenuation of dynamism into empty form and the deadening and anesthesization of everything.[14]

Having described the external effects on the world produced by the perpetrator of the color symbolism. Kovel goes on to describe the internal effects of this symbolism on the white psyche. Thus he says: [15]

> Black and white are only representations of mankind split within and between itself. The split, conceptualized psychologically in the mental structures of the id, ego and superego, is realized—as it must be—in the historical and racist world created by the ego. An inner split cannot exist without an outer one. Disjoined, separated from men and from nature, the ego sees true, living colors as 'but subtle deceits, not actually inherent in substances, but only laid on from without.'

Thus the Western psyche is schizophrenic, that is, split, for the ego is separated from the id from which it flees. This results in an abstraction which is then projected into everything that is considered the nonself: nature, making of it a "harlot" to be used, wasted, deadened; and nonwhites made invisible.[16]

Erich Neumann, another white psychologist, directly traces Western racism as a flight from the unconscious to the Christian ethic of struggle against original sin symbolized by the dark side of nature.[17]

According to Neumann, the old Judaeo-Christian ethic is based on *scapegoat psychology*. Scapegoat psychology is the result of guilt-feelings or unconscious psychic conflicts of groups and masses. In order to resolve these guilt feelings, "Evil is recognised as belonging to the collective structure of one's own tribe and is eliminated in a collective manner—for example by the High Priest transferring the sins of the people to the scapegoat as a vicarious sacrifice." [18] Neumann here uses Jung's framework, in which guilt feelings are related to the existence of the *shadow* or the unconscious. The self, on the other hand, is identified with the persona (mask) or facade personality. The result is that "the individual is now essentially split into a world of values, with which he is required to identify himself, and a world of anti-values, which are a part of his nature and can in fact be overwhelmingly strong, and which oppose the world of consciousness and values in the shape of the powers of darkness."[19]

The old ethic, observes Neumann, becomes a principle of opposites in conflict—the fight between good and evil, light and darkness. He adds:[20]

> The dualism of the old ethic, which is specially marked in its Iranian, Judaeo-Christian and Gnostic forms, divides both man, the world, and the Godhead into two tiers—an upper and a lower man, an upper and a lower world, a God and a Devil. This dichotomy is effective on the practical level in spite of all philosophical, religious or metaphysical declarations of ultimate monism. The actual situation of Western man has been essentially conditioned by this dichotomy right up to the present day.

The scapegoat psychology constitutes one of the gravest perils confronting mankind. As Neumann elucidates:[21]

> Inside a nation, the aliens who provide the objects for this projection are the minorities; if these are of a different racial or ethnological complexion, or, better still, of a different colour, their suitability for this purpose is particularly obvious. . . . The role of the alien which was played in former times by prisoners of war or shipwrecked mariners is now being played by the Chinese, the Negroes, and the Jews.

The ironic thing about the scapegoat psychology is the belief that acts committed against scapegoats are moral, even done zealously in the name of God. Thus, as Neumann observes: "True to the basic principle of the scapegoat psychology, the conscious mind believes itself to be identical with the higher values and commits the most appalling atrocities in the sublime self-assurance of an 'absolutely clear conscience'. All wars (and in particular, all wars of religion), all class wars and all party conflicts provide examples of this coexistence between a good conscience in the conscious mind and a breakthrough of the shadow on the level of action." [22] As examples of this psychological law we have Puritanism, the Inquisition, the legalistic Judaism of the Pharisees and the parade-ground discipline of the Prussian mentality.[23]

The exaggerated feelings of self-righteousness are really a compensation for feelings of insecurity and inferiority which are unconscious. The feeling of inferiority, says Neumann, results in over-compensation "by a tendency to exaggerated self-vindication and will culminate in a reenforcement of the repression." [24] Neumann explains more fully: [25]

The projection of the shadow will now become systematised, and the final result will be the paranoid reactions of individuals and whole nations, whose own repressed aggressive tendencies reappear in the shape of fear of persecution at the hands of other people and of the world at large. Slogans such as the policy of encirclement, the conspiracy of the Elders of Zion, the white, black or yellow peril, the drive for world domination of capitalism or Bolshevism, etc., and all paranoid systems of this kind serve only one purpose—to repress the aggression and the shadow side of their originators.

The cultural aggression of white peoples is also explained

by Marshall McLuhan as a lack of rootedness in the depth of the unconscious. He does not, however, use the correlative terms, conscious-unconscious, but the corresponding terms *literate* Western man as opposed to tribal man. Thus, aggression is not so much to be sought at the literate or conscious level as being simply a difference in skin color but to be sought at the unconscious level. Western man is dimly aware that the Negro (tribal man) is rooted in the superior region of the unconscious, while he with his literate culture is more shallowly rooted in the realm of the conscious. McLuhan asserted in an interview conducted with *Playboy* Magazine: [26]

> The cultural aggression of white America against Negroes and Indians is not based on skin color and belief in racial superiority, whatever ideological clothing may be used to rationalize it, but on the white man's inchoate awareness that the Negro and Indian—as men with deep roots in the resonating echo chamber of discontinuous, interrelated tribal worlds—are actually psychically and socially superior to the fragmented, alienated and dissociated man of Western civilization. Such a recognition, which stabs at the heart of the white man's entire social value system, inevitably generates violence and genocide. It has been the sad fate of the Negro and the Indian to be tribal men in a fragmented culture—men born ahead of rather than behind their time.

Western man has tried to convince himself that the level of the conscious is superior to the level of the unconscious, whereas the reverse is true. The projection of this self-deception at the conscious level has taken the form of what Frantz Fanon calls Negrophobia.

Let us now consider the psychological effects of the Western view of the superiority of consciousness symbolized as light over the unconscious symbolized as dark on black peoples. Blacks brought up in Western culture are conditioned to think that their tribal rootedness in the unconscious is inferior to the literate and logical consciousness of Western man. This causes a condition of alienation, an identity crisis. According to Isaacs, "for the Negro American (and, in varying degrees, for black men elsewhere) the element of color and physical characteristics remain the core of a deep and profound identity crisis." [27] And according to Fanon, when the Negro comes in contact with the white world, his psychic structure collapses. From henceforth, the goal of his action will be the Other (the white man), for the Other alone can give him worth.[28] The trauma that results is repressed but it continues to exist in the unconscious. It is in constant watch to come back to consciousness but in a disguised form. The collapse of the psychic structure of the Negro starts at an early age. Contact with the white world starts with the schoolboy. For example, a black schoolboy from the Antilles will identify himself with the Gauls as his ancestors, with the white man who brings truth to the savages. Thus, there is a process of identification, the young Negro subjectively adopting a white man's attitude. Fanon explains this process of identification: [29]

> (The young Antillean) invests the hero, who is white with all his own aggression—at that age closely linked to sacrificial dedication, a sacrificial dedication permeated with sadism. An eight-year-old child who offers a gift, even to an adult, cannot endure a refusal. Little by little, one can observe in the young Antillean the formation and crystallization of an attitude and a way of thinking and seeing that are essentially white. When in school he had read stories of savages told by white men, he always thinks of the Senegalese.

Besides reading his schoolbooks which are all white-oriented, the young Antillean also reads comics "put together by white men for little white men." [30] Tarzan stories, Mickey Mouse, and so on, are devoured by the local children. In these magazines

> the Wolf, the Devil, the Evil Spirit, the Bad Man, the Savage are always symbolized by Negroes or Indians; since there is always identification with the victor, the little Negro, quite as easily as the little white boy, becomes an explorer, an adventurer, a missionary 'who faces the danger of being eaten by the wicked Negroes.' [31]

Describing the general psychological result to a whole people Fanon observes: [32]

> With the exception of a few misfits within the closed environment, we can say that every neurosis, every abnormal manifestation, every affective erethism in an Antillean is the product of his cultural situation. In other words, there is a constellation of postulates, a series of propositions that slowly and subtly—with the help of books, newspapers, schools and their texts, advertisements, films, radio—work their way into one's mind and shape one's view of the world of the group to which one belongs.

We might note that what is true of the Antilles is even more true of the United States in which even the preschool Negro is exposed to one of the most powerful mediums of conditioning, television. Thus, watching a western, blacks catch themselves unconsciously encouraging and supporting the white man against the antagonist, in this case a black man or an Indian. This conditioning takes place at all levels of value, both secular and religious. At the religious level, Bastide notes: [33]

The worst was to happen when the descendants of the slaves finally assimilated North American values and gave themselves over to a "white narcissism." They could see no other way to demonstrate their identification with America than by adopting a kind of Puritanism. The introduction of this factor into Negro Protestantism defined the religion of the colored middle class. By introducing into its religion a factor historically linked to the condemnation of the Indian and the Negro as inveterate savages, the Negro middle class introduced also its own condemnation. The Christian symbolism of color, interiorized in the Negro, gave rise to the neurophatic character, marked by a guilt complex, of the Negro middle class.

Gergen also notes that there are many incidents of Negroes themselves being negatively predisposed toward those among them with dark skin. He notes that dramatic cases of this kind are found in the literature on mental illness among Negroes. Thus he says that

investigators have noted the great frequency with which the desire to be white recurs in dreams and delusional states of hospitalized Negroes. Such patients believe that they are really white, but that their skin is dirty, dyed, or painted. Some even think that they have eaten foods that have caused their skin to darken. Other investigators have found that Negroes' self-esteem may be greatly impaired as a result of such feelings, and that accompanying self-hatred may be generalized to hatred for the entire Negro race.[34]

The general negative attitude toward the color black is not limited to mental patients among blacks themselves. Gergen notes that "among normal groups, one study has shown that three out of five Negroes feel that black is the worst color to be. Among Negro college students, light-skinned Negroes are considered more attractive." [35] Gergen also cites studies of elementary and preschool children noting that "even in the second grade, Negro children will prefer white children as friends. The Clarks have found that three-year-old Negro children will notably prefer a white doll to a brown one, feeling the white doll nicer, looks better, and has a better color. Further studies show that preschool nursery children will fail to identify themselves as Negro and will prefer to see themselves as white." [36]

Harold Isaacs notes that the attitude of total rejection of self and the identification with the aggressor was a widely shared experience among North American blacks. He cites the example of William H. Ferris, author of a two-volume study called *The African Abroad* who wanted the term *Negrosaxon* because he believed that the only means of salvation for the black man lay in his complete identification with and adoption of white Anglo-Saxonism.[37]

Having described the psychological effects of color symbolism on both blacks and whites, the question that comes up at this point is how to counteract the ill psychological effects in both of them? According to Gergen, who presupposes that the negative emotional reaction to the color black is based on universal experience, "the ultimate solution may reside in the domain of racial homogenization." [38] In the meantime, he believes that the most direct mode of offsetting the negative symbolism of black is discrimination learning in the area of color symbolism; increased knowledge concerning persons of other races, knowledge of basic similarities.[39]

Other methods proposed are mentioned by Bastide: [40]

Negroes whose skin was entirely black set out to reverse the values of the traditional Catholic iconographic system. They first invented black angels with kinky hair and flat noses. Then, prompted by a sentence in the Gospels referring to the Holy Virgin, *Niger erat sed pulchra* ("Black she was, but beautiful"), they conceived of a Black Virgin.

But Bastide notes that Christ himself was left untouched, for it was felt that to make him black would have been a sacrilege.[41] Thus, the symbolism of white as superior to black was never really surmounted. The hierarchy of color remained. Of course, sooner or later, an attempt will be made to reverse the value completely. Thus in Anglo-Saxon, Protestant North America and African colonies, the revolt of the Negro went so far as to create a Black God and a Black Christ.[42] In North America we have of recent date a book entitled *The Black Messiah* by Albert B. Cleage, Jr. which tries to reverse the symbolism of Western theology.[43] Cleage claims that the Black Nation is God's chosen people: [44]

We know that Israel was a black nation and that descendents of the original black Jews are in Israel, Africa, and the Mediterranean area today. The Bible was written by black Jews. The Old Testament is the history of black Jews. The first three gospels, Matthew, Mark, and Luke, tell the story of Jesus, retaining some of the original material which establishes the simple fact that Jesus built upon the Old Testament. Jesus was a Black Messiah. He came to free a black people from the oppression of the white Gentiles. We know this now to be a fact. Our religion, our preaching, our teachings all come from the Old Testament, for we are God's chosen people. God is working with us every day, helping find a way to freedom. Jesus tried to teach the

Nation Israel how to come together as a black people, to be brothers one with another and to stand against their white oppressors.

For Cleage, black peoples are the chosen ones of God, the white peoples the rejected ones. Thus, the conflict between light and darkness envisaged by white Christianity as a conflict between white peoples as the elect of God and blacks as the rejected ones is reversed. Cleage's method of counteracting white racism is not only destructive of human brotherhood but also destructive of blacks themselves. And even granting his claim that Israel was a black nation and that Jesus was black, he would still have to contend with the many passages in the Old Testament which use the color black as a negative symbol.

Another effort to counter the negativity of blackness in white theology is that made by James Cone in his book, *Black Theology*.[45] Basing his position mostly on the New Testament, Cone claims that Christ's Gospel is toward the poor, the oppressed and the suffering. These are the blacks. They are God's chosen people and not the white race who are in fact the Anti-Christ. Cone seems to accept the traditional symbolism of white theology in which the color black is a symbol of negative values. Thus the color black symbolizes for him the oppressed, the weak and suffering, the poor. Black is sorrow, mourning, poverty. I wonder, though, whether many blacks would accept this negative symbolism of the color black. Would the color black always mean the weak, the poor, the suffering, the oppressed? Why could it not symbolize strength, power, riches, joy, triumph? I do not believe that a black man would take kindly to Christianity if he is taught that in the scriptures the color white stands for goodness and other positive values while black stands for evil and other negative values. A black in search of a religion would have to find one in which the color black stands for positive values. For many blacks, the religion taught by Black Muslims fulfills this requirement.

Elijah Muhammad considers the Black Nation or Islam as the chosen people elected by Allah.[46] In Muhammad's eschatological teaching, the struggle is to be between the Black Nation and the Caucasian race, or the world of Islam and the world of Christianity.[47] In theory, the Nation of Islam is composed of the Negro population of the United States, but in practice and for the time being, it is composed of the followers of Elijah Muhammad.[48] The comment we made with regard to Albert Cleage's proposal to counteract white racism and restore psychological pride to black peoples is applicable here to the theological doctrine of Elijah Muhammad.

In face of the criticisms of Cleage, Cone, Muhammad and others, white theology faces a great task in relation to racism. It must show that it is not inherently racist. It cannot, on the one hand, preach that the Christian God created all men equal and loves them all as his children regardless of race and color, and, on the other, use the color black as a symbol of sin, damnation, the devil—in short, of negative values, while white is used to connote positive values.

5

BLACK AS AMBIVALENT
CROSS-CULTURAL
SYMBOL

This chapter marks the beginning of the second part of our study. In the previous chapters we attempted to show how the white Christian symbolism of color in which black is mainly negative and white mainly positive has resulted in racism. We briefly noted the attempt of black theology to reverse the symbolism by giving the color black a wholly positive meaning and white a wholly negative one. We believe, however, that this results in negative racism whose effects as in the white Christian one alienate both the victim and the perpetrator of the symbolism. To correct the white Christian symbolism, one does not assign at will the values for black and white for one has to take account of the fact that symbolisms are not wholly subjective. They are partly grounded on experience. We need to base our proposed symbolism on factual evidence, through a comparative study of the symbolisms of various cultures, a study of the symbolism of mythical experience, an understanding of ambivalence in ordinary experience, philosophy and theology.

To anticipate the result of our study of the evidence, we will attempt to show that the symbols black and white are ambivalent symbols in most cultures (chapter 5); they are ambivalent symbols of mythical and ordinary experience (chapter 6); and, on the basis of this universal experience of ambivalence, we formulate a philosophic frame of reference and meaning in which the ambivalence of black and white can be grasped (chapter 7). With this philosophic formulation of the ambivalence of the symbols black and white we are then prepared to go to the Christian scriptures and re-examine them (chapter 8). With the philosophic frame of reference, we are able to accept the passages in the scriptures in which black is positive—passages which were ignored or conveniently put aside by a mind-set that approached the scriptures with the formal logic of noncontradiction. Finally we attempt to develop a theology of blackness or darkness that does justice to the ambivalent symbolism of black in the scriptures, hence a theology of blackness that is nonracist in its implications.

Having given an outline of this second part of the study, let us now proceed to show the ambivalence of the color symbols black and white in most cultures. We aim to show: (1) that the color white is a positive symbol in most cultures and by implication that the color black is considered negative, and (2) that the color black is a positive symbol in most cultures and by implication that the color white is negative. In other words, in one and the same culture, white is both a positive and a negative symbol and black is both a positive and a negative symbol.

Now a reader of this chapter conditioned by the logic of noncontradiction might consider this very ambivalence of symbolism as prelogical, unscientific, worthless. Confronted with the ambivalence he will try to make sense out of it by destroying the ambivalence. But this is to destroy the facts, or to distort them in order to fit an a priori frame of meaning based on the logic of noncontradiction. What we should do instead is to accept the fact of ambivalence and then devise a frame of reference which can grasp ambivalence. This we shall attempt to do in chapter 7.

That ambivalence is one of the laws of color symbolism is noted by Evarts: [1]

> One of the most strongly marked laws of the symbolism of color is ambivalency, or as it was called of old, the law of opposition. That which is most intimately connected with any idea is its opposite, as good, bad; deep, high; light, dark; long, short; black, white. Red, the color of love, is also the color of hate. Yellow, the color of aspiration, is also the color of degradation. Black, the color of evil and falsehood, is also the color of wisdom, prudence, and constancy in adversity.

The ambivalence of the colors black and white is found in almost all cultures. Let us start to show first the positive symbolism of white, then the positive symbolism of black.

Starting with the Greeks and Romans, Evarts notes that: [2]

> Osiris, whom the Greeks called the luminous god, was clothed in white and wore as a mark of his divinity a white tiara. The white bull was sacred to him. His priests also wore white as did Aaron and his sons. White was the attribute of Jupiter when he was Jupiter Leuceus in Greece, and Jupiter Candidus in Rome. His priesthood wore white, and the falmen dialis was honored by being allowed the white tiara. His sacrificial victims were white, the people wore white at his feasts, and days sacred to him were marked on the calendar with white chalk. On the first of January the Roman consul, clothed in white, riding on a white horse, ascended the hill to celebrate the victory of Jupiter, God of Light, over the spirit of darkness.

Going to other cultures Evarts notes that white is also a symbol of positive values. Thus he notes: [3]

Ormuzd, the Persian deity, was supposed to be the incarnation of light, and white was sacred to him. His white tunic is still the characteristic garment worn by the Parsees. The Druids wore white garments and sacrificed white oxen, while the white mistletoe was their emblem. White was also the symbol of Brahma. It was found in Scandinavia, Germany, Mexico and among the American Indians to be used with the same mystical meaning.

Kenneth Gergen furnishes data from cultures remote from the West which thus offset the possibility of cultural diffusion or influence in symbolism coming from the West. Thus to quote at length from him: [4]

For the Chiang, a Sino-Tibetan border people, a sacred white stone is a leading feature of worship. The anthropologist studying this culture notes the people's basic tendency to equate white with goodness, and blackness with evil. Among the Mongour, descendants of the Mongols, black is the color of mourning, and white betokens good fortune. The Churches of Siberia utilize black to symbolize the *Kelets,* or evil spirits. Germaine Dieterlen has observed that for the Bambara, a West African Negro tribe, white is used to symbolize wisdom and purity of the spirit. A piece of white cloth is sometimes hung over the door of a home where the inhabitants have just made a sacrifice; white is also the regal color. The dark tones of indigo, on the other hand, connote obscenity, impurity, and sadness. Black is also identified with the North and the rainy season. Similarly, Negroes of Northern Rhodesia are observed to associate good luck with cleanness and whiteness. A hunter smears a white substance on his forehead to invoke the powers of fortune; a person who has met with disaster is said to be "black on the forehead." In Nigeria, the Nupe tribe represents bleak or frightening prospects, sorcery, or evil by black, while white implies luck and good prospects. The Yorubas, also in Nigeria, wear white when worshipping, as they believe the deities prefer white. Among the Creek Indians of North America, white betokens virtue and age, and black implies death. Although the present examination did reveal irregularities, these were extremely few and limited largely to instances in which white was associated with funeral rites. In short, the major volume of the evidence suggests widespread community in feelings about black and white.

Evidence of the common symbolism of white as positive is also taken from the social perception of skin color in Japan. Thus, Hiroshi Wagatsuma notes: [5]

Long before any sustained contact with either Caucasoid Europeans or dark-skinned Africans or Indians, the Japanese valued "white" skin as beautiful and deprecated "black" skin as ugly. Their spontaneous responses to the white skin of Caucasoid Europeans and the black skin of Negroid people were an extension of values deeply embedded in Japanese concept of beauty.

Wagatsuma notes that skin color is symbolic of spiritual values: [6]

From past to present, the Japanese have always associated skin color symbolically with other physical characteristics that signify degrees of spiritual refinement or primitiveness. Skin color has been related to a whole complex of attractive or objectionable social traits.

Wagatsuma further notes that the term "white" refers to lighter shades of their own skin color and that the term "yellow" race is not used by the Japanese themselves to describe the color of their skin but is the social perception of the West of the Chinese and the Japanese.

Our author cites from Japanese literature that "white" skin is an essential characteristic of feminine beauty in Japan since recorded time. Thus from a romantic novel of the first decade of the eleventh century is noted the following: [7]

> Her color of skin was very white and she was plump with an attractive face.

> Her color was very white and although she was emaciated and looked noble, there still was a certain fulness in her cheek.

Again, our author observes that Tamenaga Shunsui (1789-1843), a writer of the late Tokugawa period mentions white skin as the essential feature of feminine beauty: [8]

> Her hands and arms are whiter than snow.

> You are well-featured and your color is so white that you are popular among your audience.

> This courtesan had a neck whiter than snow.

A fair and light skin is also the symbol of beauty in most places. As Andre Beteille notes, "in many languages the words *fair* and *beautiful* are often used synonymously. The folk literature places a high value on fair skin color. The ideal bride, whose beauty and virtue are praised in the songs sung at marriages, almost always has a light complexion." [9] In India, the preference for light skin color is associated with blood, common ancestry, birth, and is the basis for the organization of Indian society.[10]

Harold Isaacs gives further cross-cultural evidence for the symbolism of white as positive and black as negative: [11]

During an American tour in 1959, *Les Ballets Africaines*, a dance troupe from newly-independent and highly-nationalistic Guinea, performed a dance described as traditional and even ritualistic, depicting the universal theme of the duel between good and evil. Both dancers involved were black men, the good spirit appearing dressed in a shining white tunic and headdress with white plume, and the evil demon identically dressed, only in a dead black.

Varying concepts and practices relating to the colours black and white have been attributed to different African tribes. These conventions are familiar and highly visible in other cultures and long pre-date contact with Western men, e.g., in the Chinese theatre the hero's conventional make-up is always white, the villain's always black, and the same goes for the depiction of good and bad in the art of Hindu-influenced southern Asia, and for the colouring of the *wajang,* the puppets used in the most popular of all the traditional arts of Java.

With the evidence so far given of cross-cultural similarity in the symbolism of white as positive and black as negative, the question necessarily comes up, why the dramatic uniformity in symbolism? If color symbolism is purely subjective, then we would expect diversity of emotional reaction and meaning of color from one culture to another. But why does the color black arouse and elicit a negative emotional reaction, and white, a positive one?

To defend the subjective theory of the connotative meaning of color, two explanations may be proposed for the cross-cultural uniformity. One is the common innate physiological structure of man as a knowing subject. This explanation follows the Kantian theory of knowing in which the knowing subject has innate transcendental forms and schema by which chaotic and unordered phenomena from without are schematized and ordered. According to this explanation then, "certain colors stimulate a greater number of receptor cells in the retina of the eye and, thus, in the central nervous system; these same colors absorb less heat and may, therefore, be cooler to the touch." [12] But this explanation, while it is able to explain common emotional reactions arising from difference of color brightness and saturation, is unable to explain the many differences in emotional reaction produced by the all-important dimension of hue. Nor does it explain the fact that many different emotions may be aroused by the same color over a period of time.[13]

A second theory to explain the commonality of color symbolism based on subjective factors is the principle of associative learning. Gergen explains the working of this principle: [14]

Within this latter framework certain environmental events are observed to possess the inherent capacity to produce various emotions. A full stomach may provide the newborn child with a pleasurable sensation, while a loud and unexpected noise may produce fear. Various aspects of the environment to which the initial response has been neutral may come to be associated with these more basic forms of arousal. If a mother's caress has been associated with physical satisfaction, her presence on subsequent occasions may be sufficient to elicit some form of pleasure. While colors may initially be effectively neutral for the developing child, they are constant aspects of his environment. If a given color is usually present when the child is frightened or sad, through processes of associative learning such a color may come to elicit such feelings at later points in time. These associations may develop prior to linguistic abilities; unless extinguished, they may continue through the individual's life.

This theory of associative learning does not explain sufficiently, however, how peoples with highly dissimilar cultural backgrounds should react similarly to the specific colors of black and white. We have ruled out the possibility of cultural diffusion which cannot explain the germination of common associations in more isolated areas of the world.

A more adequate explanation for the commonality of color symbolism among various cultures than the purely subjective one is the objective one, namely, the presence of factors of experience that are more or less common to all cultures. In his study of primitive mythology, Joseph Campbell notes that "the diurnal alternation of light and dark" which is an ineluctable factor of experience gives rise to the polarity of light and darkness. Let us hear him explain the point: [15]

> Dawn, and awakening from this world of dream, must always have been associated with the sun and sunrise. The night fears and night charms are dispelled by light, which has always been experienced as coming from above and as furnishing guidance and orientation. Darkness, then, and weight, the pull of gravity and the

dark interior of the earth, of the jungle, of the deep sea, as well as certain extremely poignant fears and delights, must for millenniums have constituted a firm syndrome of human experience, in contrast to the luminous flight of the world-awakening solar sphere into and through immeasurable heights. Hence a polarity of light and dark, above and below, guidance and loss of bearings, confidence and fears (a polarity that we all know from our own tradition of thought and feeling and can find matched in many parts of the world) must be reckoned as inevitable in the way of a structuring principle of human thought. . . . It is a general and very deeply known experience.

Kenneth Gergen also observes that "the experience of black and white is established at a very early age, and as a result of almost universal experience." He gives two examples of such experiences: [16]

Two such experiences seem especially germane: the meaning of night versus day for the child, and the training he receives in cleanliness. Night is often a period in which the child is in isolation, without comfort or bodily gratification. Moreover, night is a perfect screen on which he can project his worst fears. Any phantom, no matter how formidable, can exist within the amorphous cover of blackness. . . . With the coming of daylight, family and environment are again visibly present, and sustenance and touch available. It is also much more difficult to project one's fears onto the compelling properties of visually apparent objects. John Dollard and Neal Miller have perhaps best outlined the profound significance of cleanliness training in the life of the child. It is unnecessary to review the details of their arguments to appreciate that for most children immersion in dirt or other dark substances is ultimately reprehensible, and unsoiled skin rewarded.

Other experiences may not be as universal as those so far mentioned but wide enough to be common among some cultures. Thus the experiential basis for the negative symbolism of black or darkness among the Semites—namely, the fear of night occasioned by the activities of thieves and robbers under cover of darkness to which they as a nomadic people were constant prey [17]—could be the basis also for a negative symbolism of darkness in other nomadic cultures.

So far we have indicated only the negative universal experience of darkness. But there is also a positive universal experience of darkness. However this experience is not as apparent to modern man as the negative experience for it is at a deeper level—the level of myth and archetypal symbols—which modern man has lost contact with. But to early man in touch with myth and archetypal symbols, darkness was experienced as positive. This experience of positive darkness came with the growth to adulthood. At an early age, the child fears darkness, hence it is a negative experience. But as he grows to adulthood he must give up the structure of the childhood personality. This process of growing up is seen as a rebirth. Thus in puberty rites, rebirth is represented as a going back to the darkness of the womb. This experience of darkness is not so much a negative experience of the absence of light as the positive one of experiencing darkness as a force, as a hidden dark energy.[18] This experience of darkness as positive is widespread for as Campbell notes: [19]

In archaic art, the labyrinth—home of the child-consuming Minotaur—was represented in the figure of a spiral. . . . It is a prominent device, furthermore, at the silent entrances and within dark passages of the ancient Irish kingly burial mound of New Grange. These facts suggest that a constellation of images denoting the plunge and dissolution of consciousness in the darkness of non-being must have been employed intentionally, from an early date, to represent the analogy of threshold rites to the mystery of entry of the child into the womb for birth. . . .

It is obvious that the idea of death-and-rebirth, rebirth through ritual and with a fresh organization of profoundly impressed sign stimuli, is an extremely ancient one in the history of culture, and that everything was done . . . to inspire in the youngsters being symbolically killed a reactivation of their childhood fear of the dark. The psychological value of such a "shock treatment" for the shattering of a no longer wanted personality structure appears to have been methodically utilized . . . for the conversion of babes into men.

Another widespread experience of darkness as positive in early cultures is the experience of the numinous. How early man actually experienced the divine is unknown to us moderns. But that he experienced it as darkness can be known from the symbol he used for such an experience. Thus he used the darkness of the womb as a symbol of mystery—the mystery of God and of eternity.[20] One is reborn from this world that is light to the darkness beyond. Early man found his God in dreams and he symbolized this by the unconscious state of the life in the womb.

From these positive experiences of darkness symbolizing the experience of the numinous, we can see somehow the reason for the uniformity in the association of black with the divine and the sacred. Let us now therefore consider the commonality of symbolism of black as positive. According to Godfrey Higgins, "Black was the sacred color of the ancient Egyptians." [21] And he states: "We have found the black complexion or something related to it whenever we have approached the origin of nations. The Alma Mater, the Goddess Multimammia, the founders of oracles: the Memnon or first idols were always black." [22]

Even for the Ancient Greeks in their pre-philosophic age when consciousness and logic were not overemphasized and the world was still experienced in a sacral and mythological way, black was also seen as a symbol of the divine. As Higgins observes: [23]

> In my search for the origin of the Ancient Druids I continually found, at last, that my labours terminated with something black. Thus the oracles of Dodona and of Apollo at Delphi were founded by Black Doves. Doves are not often, I believe, never black. Osiris and his Bull were black; all the Gods and Goddesses of Greece were black, at least this was the case with Jupiter, Bacchus, Hercules, Apollo, Ammon. The Goddesses Venus, Isis, Hecate, Juno, Metis, Ceres, Cybele were black in the Campodoglio at Rome.

When consciousness and logic were emphasized, this resulted in the diminution of the imaginative and artistic faculties instrumental in achieving and preserving archetypal symbols.[24]

If we now go to the nonwestern cultures of both the Old and New Worlds, we also find the color black as symbol of the divine. The Cambridge Encyclopedia shows that the earliest Messiahs were depicted as dark-skinned and with wooly hair: Thus, in India in 1366 B.C. we have the first Buddha who was foretold by prophets as the Messiah; he was the son of the Holy Spirit and the Virgin, Maia, born in the village of Rajagriha, recognized and worshipped by wise men; a messianic star stood over the place of his nativity. His complexion was black; his hair woolly.[25]

In Egypt, 1350 B.C., the God Osiris was sun-rayed; his complexion was black and his hair was woolly. Again in India, 1332 B.C., was the birth of Ies Christna, the ninth incarnation of Vishnu. This Christna had a black complexion and his hair was woolly. In Japan in 1000 B.C. during the era of Buddha, the Buddha was represented as in most other images as with woolly hair. In India in 721 B.C., the era of the nativity of Buddha, this son of Maya was born among shepherds to the accompaniment of flowers, music and perfumes, had a black complexion and his hair was woolly. In China, 667 B.C., the era of Lao-kuin or Lao-tsze, we have Lao-tsze who was a divine incarnation in human form, born of a virgin black in complexion and as beautiful as jasper.[26]

In the New World, black complexion is also common among statues of the gods. Thus, in Mexico, 722 A.D., Quetzalcoatl who was recognized as the Messiah by seers and astrologers had a complexion that was black and hair that was woolly.[27] Another Mexican god, Ixtlilton, is a Negro god, for the very term itself means blackfaced.[28] In Ecuador, a statuette estimated to be 20,000 years old is that of a Negro. And "some statues of the Indian gods in Central America possess typical Negro features and certain prehistoric monuments there undoubtedly represent Negroes." [29]

Another Central American god, "The Black Christ," has an image in the little church at Esquipultas, in Guatemala, to which thousands of Indians journey annually from all parts of Central America and even from Mexico and South America. As A. Hyatt Verril, an observer and noted authority on the Central American Indian has remarked, "to all outward intents and purposes they (pilgrims) are Christians making a pilgrimage to a Christian Church in order to worship before a figure of Christ. No doubt many of them are sincere in believing this to be the case. But as a matter of fact the underlying cause, the real urge that leads them to the spot is the ineradicable faith in their ancient gods and religion. The very fact that the image is black has a symbolic significance. Moreover, among many of the Indians, the Black Christ is referred to in private as Ekchuah." [30] Ekchuah, the black god, was the special deity of merchants and cacao planters.

So far we have been showing evidence of the positive symbolism of black. This evidence counter-balanced the previous one in which white was seen as positive and black as negative. Let us now go to the continent of Africa to illustrate the ambivalence of the colors black and white. From a very exhaustive study of the concepts of God in Africa, John S. Mbiti has found that some peoples consider black as a color sacred to God so that in their sacrifices, only black animals are offered. On the other hand, there are also other peoples for whom white is the color of superhuman powers such that white animals and white articles only are offered. Thus, the Basoga, Bavenda, Butawa, Luo, Meru, Nandi, Ndebele, Sandawe, Sebei, and Shona peoples sacrifice or offer black animals and items, for example black dogs, sheep, oxen, goats, cows. In contrast, the Abaluyia, Ganda, Gofa and Watumbatu peoples offer white hens, goats, cocks, cows and other white items. For the Ganda, white is regarded as the color of superhuman powers and they use it in sacred rituals; the Itsekiri "tie a white cloth or chicken at the end of their forked bamboo staff which seems to serve as an altar." [31]

The colors black and white symbolize not only things sacred to God as we have seen above but also God himself. Mbiti notes that "according to one Maasai myth, there were originally four gods, of whom the black was 'very good', the white was 'good', the blue was 'neither good nor bad', and the red was 'bad'." [32] Here we do not have the dichotomy present in white theology in which God is symbolized by light or white alone. In the myth both white and black are symbolic of divinity. We can speculate why the myth considers the black god very good and the white god only good. It might be proferred as an explanation that God is imaged according to the eye of the beholder which in this case is black. But the more probable explanation is that for the native mind since the normal way in which God is met or experienced is through dreams, he is therefore symbolized by darkness more generally than white. Thus according to the Nuba people "God comes to their rainmakers at night in dreams." [33] Thus, observes Mbiti, night is a symbol of time for communication and contact with God. Black, however, is not always a positive symbol. For example for the Vugusu people, black symbolizes evil divinity and for the Galla people God is referred to as black when the sky is overcast. And the "Dinka divinity believed to be the final explanation of sufferings and misfortunes, is known as 'the Great Black one' ".[34] These negative symbolisms, however, seem to be more the exception than the rule. In general black is a positive symbol of the divine. But from this we cannot infer that white is a symbol of evil, for as we noted in the Maasai myth the white god is also a good god. Some African peoples use white as a symbol of God. Thus the Gikuyu address God as "the Possessor of Whiteness." The Yoruba "speak of God as 'the Pure King', 'the One clothed in white robes, who dwells above', and 'Whiteness without patterns (absolutely white), essentially white object. . . . To distinguish God from other spiritual beings, the Vugusu refer to him as 'the White God' ".[35]

From a study of the symbolism of black and white in Africa, the Western mind might conclude that it is full of contradictions. This conclusion follows from the Western mind-set based on the principle of noncontradiction or identity. But the native mentality has a logic all its own which is not Western so that what is contradictory to the Western mind is not necessarily so to the native mind.[36] In the next chapters we will show in a more formal and philosophic way how it is possible for black to symbolize both positive and negative experiences and values and how the myth-oriented mentality may have after all a more profound grasp of the divine than the logical and scientific mind.

But even in the westernized approach to the Judaeo-Christian religion, something of the ambivalence of the symbolism of black and white found in the origins of this religion has survived the purging of these so-called contradictions instituted by the Platonic and Aristotelian theologies of the Christian Church. As we have noted in the earlier chapters, Western symbolism uses black to symbolize evil, sin, and white to symbolize goodness, grace and salvation, such that in accordance with this symbolism, Western religious practice went to the extreme of even bleaching the skins of Jesus and Mary. But the worship of the Black Virgin and Child in many parts of Europe cannot be ignored. As George Higgins has observed: [37]

In all the Romish countries of Europe, in France, Italy, Germany, etc., the God, Christ, as well as his Mother is described in the old pictures to be black. The infant God in the arms of his black mother, his eyes and drapery white, is, himself, perfectly black. If the reader doubts my word he may go to the Cathedral at Moulins—to the famous Chapel of the Virgin of Loretto, to the Church of the Annunciata; the Church of St. Lazaro, or the Church of St. Stephen at Genoa; to St. Francisco at Pisa; to the Church at Brixen in the

Tyrol, and that at Padua; to the Church of St. Theodore at Munich, in the last two of which the whiteness of the eyes and teeth and the studied redness of the lips are observable; to a church and to the Cathedral at Augsburg, where are a Black Virgin and Child as large as life; to the Borghese Chapel, Maria Maggiore; to the Pantheon; to a small Chapel of St. Peter's on the right hand side on entering near the door; and, in fact to almost innumerable other churches in countries professing the Romish religion.

George Higgins also observes that "very often the black figures have given way to white ones and in these cases the black ones, as being held sacred, were put in retired places in the churches, but were not destroyed, and are yet to be found there." [38] Now, when the circumstance of these black images and their profound veneration by the illiterate masses was brought to the attention of the priests, Higgins noted that "they have endeavored to disguise the fact by pretending that the child had become black by the smoke of the candles." [39] But Higgins comments that the image was "black where the smoke of the candle never came; and besides how came the candles not to blacken the white teeth and the shirt, and how came they to redden the lips?" [40]

The exact origin of the Black Christ and Black Madonna is not known. Higgins believes that the black icon of Christ he saw in Italy came there even before the foundation of the Rome of Romulus. And C. W. King says that "the Black Virgins so highly venerated in certain French cathedrals during the long night of the Middle Ages, proved when at last examined by antiquarian eyes to be basalt statues of the Egyptian Goddess, which having merely changed the name continued to receive more than pristine adoration." [41] And Gerald Massey in his book, *Ancient Egypt* notes that: [42]

The black Jesus is a well-known form of the child-Christ worshipped on the continent (Europe) where the black Bambino was the pet image of the Italian church as popular as Crishna, the Black Christ of India; and unless the divine son was incarnated in black flesh, the type of the black child must have survived from the black Iu, the black Kak or Jack, the black Sut Nahsi, the Negro image of the earliest God.

Some of the images according to Higgins "particularly the Madonnas of Constuchan in Tolers and the Mother of God statue in Alt-Olting in Bavaria near Munich, were brought from Palestine more than 1,000 years ago by Ritter von Heiligers Lande." [43]

In the great mystical tradition of the West darkness is a symbol of the divine as when Dionysius the Areopagite speaks of God as the Divine Darkness.[44]

In Western literature, black and white are likewise ambivalent colors. Thus we noted how Milton mentioned black as the hue of Wisdom, while Shakespeare and Shelley spoke of the whiteness of death.[45] Evarts mentions other uses of the color white as a negative symbol:[46]

Showing the white feather is a confession of cowardice which borrows its metaphor from the fact that game-cocks should have no white feathers. White feathers indicate cross breeding in fowls, and the gamester so bred would not have so high a fighting spirit. Having a white elephant on our hands is a figurative way of speaking of having a burdensome dignity to support. It comes to us from Siam, the land where the white elephant is sacred and must be cared for with all due pomp and ceremony. If the monarch wishes to ruin anyone he presents him with a white elephant and the resultant expense soon rids him of the objectionable family. White is the color of sickness and of death because of the absence of the hue of life.

We conclude this chapter on the cross-cultural ambivalence of the color symbols black and white by noting that even in Western culture, at least, in its early beginnings, the ambivalence of the colors black and white was present. The modern logical and rational mind, however, has forgotten this ambivalence. To grasp the ambivalency of black and white, the modern rational and logical mind needs to return to its past. This is the task to be done in the next chapter.

6

BLACK AS AMBIVALENT
SYMBOL OF EXPERIENCE

Our over-all task in the second part of our study is the opening up to the modern rationalistic and logical mind [1] certain dimensions of human experience in which the color black could be accepted as a carrier of positive value and meaning: for, as our previous chapters have shown, the modern logical and scientific mind has lost the positive experience of blackness or darkness. We have seen the extremism with respect to human relations which has resulted from the loss of the positive experience of darkness. The task then for modern Western thought is to arrive at a synthesis both in theory and in practice that includes the positive experience of darkness.[2] As the noted psychologist Erich Neumann has remarked, "The acceptance of darkness as positive will lead to an inner form of humanization which is not merely a knowledge of logic and concepts but an experience of the whole man, a return to primal beginnings." [3]

The particular task of this chapter is to show the ambivalence of black at the mythical level and at the ordinary level of experience.[4] Let us start with mythical experience.

Mythical experience is best exemplified by the experience

of primal or early man.[5] Mythical experience is an experience of what we would call today the realm of the unconscious. Experience of the unconscious is expressed through archetypal symbols which are ambivalent for they express the ambivalent experience of the unconscious. Thus, as Erich Neumann notes, in the early beginnings of a nation's culture when archetypal symbols were operative, we find the symbol appearing "as an original and natural unity, containing positive and negative elements, darkness and light." [6]

Modern scientific and rational experience, in contrast, is confined almost exclusively to the realm of the conscious. As Neumann observes, Western man overemphasizes consciousness. Instead of an integrated symbol that unifies light and darkness, he has a fragmented symbol in which black or darkness is evil; light or whiteness good. He has failed to see the goodness of darkness. As a result, Western consciousness has been a flight from darkness. Hence, it has been a flight from the realm of the unconscious, the region of myth and archetypal symbols, to the region of consciousness, the sphere of concepts and definitions.

Early man's experience of the realm of the unconscious is described by Neumann thus: [7]

Human life in the beginning is determined to a far higher degree by the unconscious than by consciousness; it is directed more by archetypal images than by concepts, by instincts than by the voluntary decisions of the ego; and man is more a part of his group than an individual. And similarly, his world is not a world seen by consciousness, but one experienced by the unconscious. In other words, he perceives the world not through the functions of consciousness, as an objective world presupposing the separation of subject and object, but experiences it mythologically, in archetypal images, in symbols that are a spontaneous expression of the unconscious, that help the psyche orient itself in the world, and that, as mythological motifs, configure the mythologies of all peoples.

Both mythic and rational man look upon the region of the unconscious as darkness, as black. The difference is that the former sees darkness as positive and negative, hence, as ambivalent, while the latter sees only the negativity of darkness. That the unconscious is positive darkness is noted by Jung: [8]

> The dream is a little hidden door in the innermost and most secret recesses of the psyche, opening into that cosmic night which was the psyche long before there was any ego consciousness, and which will remain psyche no matter how far our ego consciousness may extend. . . . All consciousness separates; but in dreams we put on the likeness of that more universal, truer, more eternal man dwelling in darkness of primordial night.

For rational and logical modern man, ego consciousness is trusted to bring psychic integration. But it causes only alienation. There in the realm of primordial night will modern man find wholeness.

From the mystical point of view, the dark world of the unconscious furnishes an experience of the divine as energy and force whereas the light world of waking consciousness gives only the experience of death. Thus, the Indian Mandukya Upanishad tells us to descend from the light world of waking consciousness to the innermost depth of the psyche for it is there that "The Knower, the Lord of All, the Omniscient, the Indwelling Controller, the Source or Generative

Womb of All: The Beginning and End of beings" is found.[9] The light world of waking consciousness which Western man mostly inhabits is described by Campbell thus: [10]

(The) objects are gross matter and are separated from each other: a is not b. Perceived by the senses, named by the mind, and experienced as desirable or fearful, they compose the world of what Goethe called "the become and the set fact: the dead," of which the understanding (Verstand) is concerned only to make use. This is the aspect of experience that Mephistopheles comprehends and controls: the world of empirical man, his desires, fears and duties, laws, statistics, economics, and "hard facts." It is the world, as Stephen Dedalus judged, of the shells left behind by life: "Crush, crack, crik, crick. Wild sea money." Money and securities, banalities and fixed forms. It is the Waste Land, Dante's Hell: the world of naturalistic art and intellectual abstraction.

From the point of view of waking consciousness its world is full while the world of the unconscious is dark, blank.[11] But the opposite is the truth. Western rational and logical man cannot attain the dark region of the unconscious by the logical method and by thinking. He must learn to use his imagination and feeling and apply the principle of paradox and the law of participation.[12]

The logical mode of thinking separates object and subject. Knowledge is by way of definition which is the setting of boundaries, the cutting off of an object, its isolation from the rest. Rational knowledge, then, is dualistic. It operates by the principle of identity or noncontradiction. It is analytic rather than synthetic. In other words, to know a thing is to reduce it to its basic elements: atomic impressions as the unit

of knowledge as in the empirical school, or atomic propositions as in modern linguistic analysis. Analysis is the method
par excellence of science.

In general, we might say that the rational and logical
mind is more analytic than synthetic, while the native mind
is more synthetic than analytic. This distinction, however, is
not exactly correct, for synthesis with respect to native thinking is not to be taken in the sense of unifying concepts or
impressions by simple association or by the application of the
principle of causality. Natives have, instead, collective representations which are not, like concepts, the result of intellectual processes [13] that relate the knower to the object objec-
tively. Rather, they contain as integral parts, affective and
motor elements.[14] Collective representations are both themselves and other than themselves. As Lévy-Bruhl notes, "the
opposition between the one and the many, the same and
another, and so forth, does not impose upon this mentality
the necessity of affirming one of the terms if the other is
denied, or vice versa." [15]

Natives see many things in the sense data of which we
are unconscious. "The object is not merely discerned by
the mind in the form of an idea or image; according to the
circumstances of the case, fear, hope, religious awe, the
need and the ardent desire to be merged in one common
essence, the passionate appeal to a protecting power—these
are the soul of these representations, and make them at
once cherished, formidable, and really *sacred* to the ini-
tiated." [16] Lévy-Bruhl observes that "the profound difference
which exists between primitive mentality and our own is shown
even in the ordinary perception or mere apprehension of the
very simplest things. Primitive perception is fundamentally
mystic on account of the mystic nature of the collective representations which form an integral part of every perception." [17] We have lost the sense of the sacred, the sense of
identity and oneness with nature which the natives had. And

we think that this is progress for we incorrectly think that natives "associate occult powers, magic properties, a kind of soul or vital principle with all the objects which affect their senses or strike their imagination, and that their perceptions are surcharged with animistic beliefs. . . . It is not a question of *association*. The mystic properties with which things and beings are imbued form an integral part of the idea to the primitive, who views it as a synthetic whole." Thus, natives "see with eyes like ours but they do not perceive with the same minds." [18]

We have an aversion to mysticism as implying occult powers, magic properties. But the term mystic expressed in modern knowledge means that the native is related to reality more in terms of the unconscious dimension of his mind than by the conscious. The native believes in forces and influences from the world outside which though imperceptible to consciousness and to sense are nevertheless real [19] as affecting the deeper dimension of the unconscious. It is at the level of the unconscious in which the principle of noncontradiction is nonoperative and in which what Lévy-Bruhl calls the law of participation is operative.[20] The natives' collective representations derive from the region of the unconscious and are therefore suffused and surrounded by the mystical, the emotional. These are more important than the attributes of which our senses inform us.[21]

Why cannot we accept the possibility that man is related to reality in deeper ways than mere consciousness and that perhaps this unconscious relation affects man in a much more profound way than conscious knowledge? Is this not perhaps the insight of the native mentality? And if he cannot be logical is it not because of the nature of the experience at the level of the unconscious which cannot be expressed conceptually, logically, and for which he uses symbols, instead?

Another insight of the native mentality which we are only

now beginning to accept is the importance of dreams. To the modern mind, dreams are unreal compared to conscious thinking. But as Lévy-Bruhl notes, to the natives, the dream "is of far greater significance than to us. It is first a precept as real as those of the waking state, but above all it is a provision of the future, a communication and intercourse with spirits, souls, divinities, a means of establishing a relation with their own special guardian angel, and even of discovering who this may be." [22] Now, if we accept the region of the unconscious as more important than the level of the conscious, then dreams take on great significance. Mystics have indicated that the unconscious is the region of archetypal symbols, of the divine. This is true for the native mentality. As Lévy-Bruhl notes, "But in whatsoever fashion the dream may be conceived, it is always regarded as a sacred thing, and as the most usual method employed by the gods of making their will known to men." [23] From the belief of natives that God appears in the darkness of sleep, perhaps we can get some indication why God is almost always symbolized by darkness as we noted in the previous chapter. God appears in the region of the unconscious, rather than at the level of consciousness.

The view of Erich Neumann we noted in the early part of this chapter that Western man must return to primal beginnings is also noted by a North American thinker, Marshall McLuhan. McLuhan sees three stages in man's development corresponding to and being a function of the means of communication. Thus, just as there have been three stages in communication, the oral, the literate and the electric, so three ages of man, the preliterate or tribal, the literate or logical, and the retribalized man.[24]

In the West, according to McLuhan, literate or logical culture causes a fragmentation in thought and life causing specializations, division of functions, of social classes, of nations, of knowledge. Because of this fragmentation, the rich interplay of all the senses that characterized the tribal society is sacrificed.[25] With the emphasis on sight as the model for knowing, the visual or conscious was overemphasized and the aural or the unseen deemphasized. Again here, the analysis of Neumann is supported that Western man overemphasizes consciousness and depreciates the unconscious.

In contrast to Western man, tribal man "was not differentiated by his specialist talents or his visible characteristics, but by his unique emotional blends. The internal world of the tribal man was a creative mix of complex emotions and feelings that literate men of the Western world have allowed to wither or have suppressed in the name of efficiency and practicality." [26] Instead of being visually oriented, tribal man was aural: "The man of the tribal world led a complex, kaleidoscopic life precisely because the ear, unlike the eye, cannot be focused and is synaesthetic rather than analytical and linear. Speech is an utterance, or more precisely, an *outering,* of all our senses at once; the auditory field is simultaneous, the visual successive." [27] As a result of the aural orientation of tribal man "the modes of life of nonliterate people were implicit, simultaneous and discontinuous, and also far richer than those of literate man. By their dependence on the spoken word for information, people were drawn together into a tribal mesh; and since the spoken word is more emotionally laden than the written—conveying by intonation such rich emotions as anger, joy, sorrow, fear—tribal man was more spontaneous and passionately volatile. Audile-tactile tribal man partook of the collective unconscious, lived in a magical integral world patterned by myth and ritual, its values divine and unchallenged, whereas literate or visual man creates an environment that is strongly fragmented, individualistic, explicit, logical, specialized and detached." [28]

Fragmentation and alienation, the result of literate cul-

destrian personalities whose capacity for vision and ecstasy is sadly crippled. It has resulted in a deformed man whose sense of a mysterious origin and cosmic destiny has nearly disappeared. A race that has lost touch with past and future through the debilitation of ritual, revelry, and visionary aspirations will soon shrink to a tribe of automatons.

To the naive, a return to primal beginnings or retribalization means a return to earthly deities, witchcraft and "black" magic. But its true meaning is that the return is a recovery of atrophied faculties early man possessed so as to be able to relate more deeply to nature, other peoples and to himself. A return to the "Africa within" means an appreciation of the dimension of the unconscious as the source of hidden dark energy.[34] It means an appreciation of darkness as a positive symbol. The healing of the one-sidedness or extremism of rational and logical consciousness as Jung suggests is for ego-consciousness to cease becoming the center of its valuation and construction and to submit to the unconscious as the center of its organization.[35]

A return to the positive darkness of the unconscious is also the message of Norman O. Brown, who by combining the great insight of Nietzsche and of Freudian psychology, sees the task of Western man as the construction of a Dionysian ego. Thus he says: [36]

The human ego must face the Dionysian reality, and therefore a great work of self-transformation lies ahead of it. For Nietzsche was right in saying that the Apollonian preserves, the Dionysian destroys, self-consciousness. As long as the structure of the ego is Apollonian, Dionysian experience can only be bought at the price of ego-dissolution. Nor can the issue be resolved by a 'synthesis' of the Apollonian and the Dionysian; the problem is the construction of a Dionysian ego.

Apollo according to Nietzsche is the god of form—of plastic form in art, of rational form in thought, of civilized form in life. This form negates instinct. Apollo's world is the world of sunlight. Hence, knowing is seeing forms, perceiving but not tasting. This type of knowing flees from darkness, from the instinct as nonrational. Hence, Apollo is the god who sustains "displacement from below (darkness) upward (light)." [37] Brown observes that Plato who gave us the theory and philosophy of eternal forms is the son of Apollo.

Dionysus, on the other hand, is the real world as opposed to the world of appearance. Dionysus is "drunkenness; not life kept at a distance and seen through a veil but life complete and immediate." He is "the image of the instinctual reality which psychoanalysis will find on the other side of the veil." In Freudian terms, Dionysus symbolizes the id in which there is no negation, only affirmation and eternity. Dionysus "affirms the dialectical unity of the great instinctual opposites: Dionysus reunifies male and female, Self and Other, life and death." [38] And we might add that it reunifies light and darkness, black and white.

The present predicament of Western man according to Brown which is cumulative repression, guilt and aggression, is due to the overemphasis of the Apollonian or rather the construction of the Western ego on the Apollonian (form, light, appearance) which follows and operates by the formal logical law of contradiction, a law that is unable to unify opposites.

Western man does not have to go back to other cultures to recover the mystical dimension. All he has to do is to go back to the beginnings of Western culture, for, as Brown notes, "the Greeks, who gave us Apollo, also gave us the alternative, Nietzsche's Dionysus." [39]

So far we have been showing that the dark unconscious unifies both light and darkness. Black as a color symbol of the unconscious is thus an ambivalent symbol. Now, we would like to show that even at the level of ordinary experience, black is an ambivalent symbol signifying both positive and negative values.

Let us discuss first the negative emotional experience of darkness and later the positive one. According to Kenneth Gergen, whom we cited earlier, the negative emotional response to the experience of black or darkness and conversely the positive emotional response to the experience of light or white are established at an early age based on almost universal human experience. Gergen mentions two ordinary experiences: the experience of night and day, and the experience of cleanliness as opposed to dirt.[40] For the child, night is the period of isolation, without comfort from the mother, without bodily gratification. Fear is the basic emotional experience associated with darkness. This negative emotional experience of fear is true not only for the child but also for the adult as noted by Wallace Steven's poem "Domination of Black": [41]

I saw the night come,
Come striding like the color of the heavy hemlocks.
I felt afraid.

In contrast to the negative experience of night as fearful is the positive experience of day as evoking joy and happiness for once again the mother is present and security and sustenance are once more available.

The same emotions of fear or joy are evoked by dirt and cleanliness respectively. Dirt repels, cleanliness attracts. The child is hugged when clean, left alone when dirty. Dirt is a blot, spot, hence black, dark, while cleanliness is spotlessness, hence, white.

As we noted earlier, it is not the infant alone who experiences darkness as negative and white as positive but also the adult. Even with the advance in technology, darkness or night is still associated with fear: fear of danger at home or out in the streets. Nighttime is associated with killing, burglary and other crimes. Night is associated with craftiness and the hatching of diabolical plots.

Night or darkness is also associated with the imagination; day or light with seeing. Night is formless, hence the region of phantoms. Day, on the other hand, is the region of visually apparent forms or objects. Objects that are seen do not provoke fear of the unknown. Night is associated with the imagination, for it is at night that the imagination is most active, forming images that become frightful precisely because they are not controlled by real facts or forms. "Night is a perfect screen on which a person can project his worst fears." [42] Phantoms appear causing nightmares. Night is also associated with the devil who works his machinations in the dark, unseen. On the other hand, reason, as opposed to the imagination, is associated with light or day. Through the light of reason we are able to see objects, hence we are brought back to reality and to the familiar. It is imagination that enslaves and oppresses, that creates the spook and the bogeyman who are, of course, black as night. The ordinary negative experience of night and darkness is generalized to cover all dark or black objects, hence, black peoples are often referred to as spooks, bogeymen. As the fear of night and darkness, so the fear of black peoples, otherwise known as Negrophobia.

It is not necessary to dwell long on the negative emotional responses associated with darkness or night for we have described in chapter 1 many instances of these responses based on the ordinary experience of night and darkness of the Hebrew peoples. Let us consider now some positive emotional responses deriving from the experience of night or darkness.

The positive emotional responses to night or darkness come later in the development of the child, as it conquers the fear of night.

Night, from nature's point of view, is the time for growth, hence life and being, not death. In the ordinary experience of mankind, night is the time for sexual union, hence, it is the time of creativity, joy, ecstasy. Day, in contrast, is the time of labor, sweat, suffering, hence, it connotes loss of energy. Day is entropic, that is, it is a process of dying. Night, by way of contrast, is the time of rest, hence, renewal, rejuvenation, the source of energy.

If these positive emotional experiences of darkness or night are not as apparent to most people as the negative ones, perhaps the reason is that it requires a little more reflection on one's experience than the negative experiences, a condition which most people engrossed with day-to-day living do not have. A little more reflection will show, however, that darkness or night does evoke positive emotional reactions.

Let us pursue further the experience of night or darkness as energy or potency. A little reflection will show that darkness as in the darkness of the earth or of the soil implies fertility, potency, energy, whereas whiteness as in a light soil or the "white" sands of the desert implies barrenness, aridity, lifelessness. Again, the blackness of coal implies hidden energy and so is the center of the sun, the source of light energy, a fiery seething darkness.

A positive reaction to darkness as potency and fertility is also derived from the experience of human sexuality. Sexuality is often associated with the darkness of night as being the time when sexual union is ordinarily and frequently performed. It is possible that the belief of both whites and blacks that black is more potent than white [43] is partly derived from the association of night with sexuality, growth, and fertility. And the sexual mystique of blacks being more sexually potent than whites [44] may be due to the transference of the symbolism of black as potency and energy to peoples with dark skins. But it could also be due to the association of black peoples in the minds of whites with the beastly,[45] the instinctive, as opposed to the rational and logical. These two explanations for the belief in the sexual potency of black peoples are not really unrelated, for as we noted earlier, the instinctive and the imaginative are related to night or darkness while reason is related to the daytime when objects are seen. Imagination and instinct are dark and inferior as being associated with animals, while reason is light, that is, a seeing faculty, and is associated with the human.

But in another sense, imagination is superior to reason, for as the child matures to adulthood, imagination is no longer the source of spooks and bogeymen but the source of creativity. The imagination becomes a liberator from the absolutization of the forms and shapes of the present as real by reason, for the imagination can present alternatives which conceptual reason fixed upon empirical facts only is unable to imagine. Reason solely confined to the present is imprisoned in it. Imagination becomes its liberator, for it is imagination which can transcend the present being able to attain the future, being able to envision another day free from the harshness, nastiness and brutishness of the present life.

Whiteness we noted earlier is associated with cleanliness, spotlessness and black with dirt. But from a different point of view, whiteness could connote blankness, emptiness, superficiality, while blackness could connote fullness, depth, profundity. Again purity and chastity are often symbolized by pure driven snow; impurity by darkness. But whiteness as the whiteness of winter could also mean coldness, lifelessness. Whiteness too is the symbol of death as in the deathly whiteness of a corpse and the icy coldness of death, and deathly paleness is the symbol of fear, not joy. And finally, whiteness could symbolize sin, not purity and chastity as when the whiteness of leprosy is used as a sign of sin in the scriptures.

Ordinary experiences are often the basis for theological beliefs or at least confirmations of such. For example, just as a white skin being light in color is closer in color to sunlight, so white peoples are the elect of God as being closer to God as the Divine Sun who radiates the light of grace. But from a different point of view, the analogy fails since at the physical level, a more prolonged exposure to the sun darkens the skin while a lack of exposure makes the skin pale and white. A dark skin then is a sign of closeness to rather than a sign of absence from the sun. Thus, white could mean, paradoxically, absence of light, while black could mean the fullness of light.

We speak of black skies and storm clouds as opposed to clear and cloudless skies and we use these physical facts in a metaphorical way to express aspects of the human condition. When misfortune, sorrow and suffering befall one, we speak of dark clouds in one's life and when life is happy and joyful, we speak of cloudless skies, of serene weather on life's horizon. Again, in the symbolisms just noted, black is evil and white is good. But from another point of view, constantly clear skies are not necessarily a sign of good fortune in the physical order, for such a condition is often found in the desert. Storm clouds, on the other hand, are a boon and a blessing, for they signify rain, hence, life-giving water for a verdant earth.

We believe we have given sufficient evidence for the ambivalence of both the colors black and white from mystical and ordinary experience. From this evidence we are now in a position to devise a philosophical frame of reference in which the ambivalence of the colors black and white could be better understood. This task will occupy us in the next chapter.

7

BLACK AS SYMBOL
OF REALITY AND TRUTH

I n the previous chapter we said
that Western consciousness needs
to go back to its primal begin-
nings, to recover the sense of myth and mysticism, in order
to achieve an experience of black as positive. This experience
early man had. But in the West this mystical or Dionysian
experience atrophied and in its stead the Apollonian prevailed.
The Apollonian dominance resulted in a flight from darkness,
from the id or unconscious. This flight from darkness was reenforced by the Apollonian Christian symbolism of color in
which black was the symbol of sin and evil and white of
innocence and goodness.

We suggested as the first step in the recovery of a positive
experience of darkness the realization that ordinary experiences of light and darkness and black and white are ambivalent and therefore cannot be properly grasped by the
formal logic of noncontradiction. The next step is to formulate this experience of ambivalence in a philosophic way so
that it is possible for Western man to go back to his primal
beginnings in Hellenic and Jewish thought and experience

and grasp the original experience of black as a positive symbol.

In this chapter, then, we need to have a philosophic frame of reference which is able to express black as a positive symbol of truth and reality. We need to restructure Western philosophy in such a way that the Dionysian dimension forms the basis of meaning and being, for the history of Western philosophy has been mainly Apollonian, hence not a valid frame of meaning within which to grasp the positive character of darkness. Darkness as a philosophic symbol in the Apollonian philosophic tradition is ignorance; light is knowledge. This symbolism goes all the way back to Plato, the most influential philosopher for the West. Indeed, Plato has the Dionysian dimension in his philosophy, for as F. M. Cornford has noted, Plato's philosophy is rooted in Greek religion and mythology.[1] But in the course of the historical development of Western philosophy, it was the Apollonian aspect of his philosophy—the theory of forms—that was most influential while the mythical parts of his philosophy were ignored.

Even in comparatively recent Western philosophies, the Dionysian dimension survives. To mention but two philosophies considered to be the best exponents of the Apollonian dimension, hence, antimythical and antipoetic—the philosophy of Charles Sanders Peirce, the father of pragmatism, and of Ludwig Wittgenstein, the forerunner of linguistic analysis—the Dionysian dimension lives on, although it is hidden and attenuated. For example, Charles Peirce holds that it is not mechanism and chance, the twin bulwarks of the scientific enterprise, that fully explain the dynamism of the universe but evolutionary love, hence, ultimately mysticism.[2] And Ludwig Wittgenstein in his *Tractatus Logico-Philosophicus* admits the dimension of the mystical:

Proposition 6.44 "It is not how things are in the world that is mystical, but that it exists."

Proposition 6.522 "There are, indeed, things that cannot be put into words. They make themselves manifest. They are what is mystical."

While it is true that the Dionysian dimension of reality survives in many Western philosophies, it has not been articulated in such a way as to present darkness as a positive symbol of truth and reality. If at all, darkness is a symbol of nonbeing and falsehood. I therefore try to present in this chapter a philosophy of process [3] which I believe is able to express the ambivalent symbolism of black and in so doing open up to Apollonian man the positive experience of darkness in his Hellenic and Christian past.

Let us start by recalling the symbolism of black and white, light and dark in Apollonian Western philosophy. Thus, light or white symbolizes truth, while darkness or black symbolizes ignorance and untruth. Black is also used to signify the unreal. It signifies nonbeing and death; white on the other hand stands for being and life.

At the psychological level, white stands for consciousness which is light; black for the unconscious region of the psyche which is dark. Darkness is also applied to the infrahuman levels of evolution which are in a state of unconsciousness—the mineral and plant kingdoms. They live in total darkness devoid of the light of the senses or of reason. The animal kingdom, on the other hand, has a degree of consciousness, for it has, at least in the higher forms of life, sense knowledge. But compared to human consciousness and knowledge, animal knowing is dark.

By association, the philosophical and psychological symbolism of blackness is then transferred to peoples possessing dark skins. Thus, they have dark minds; they dwell in darkness. A black skin signifies a lower level in the hierarchy of evolutionary development, hence, less developed in intelligence. At the level of the unconscious, observes Frantz Fanon, "there is the firmly fixed image of the nigger-savage." [4]

The philosophic symbolism of black as connoting inferior being is implicit in the following passage: [5]

You can dress a chimpanzee, housebreak him, and teach him to use a knife and fork, but it will take countless generations of evolutionary development, if ever, before you can convince him that a caterpillar or a cockroach is not a delicacy. Likewise, the social, political, economical, and religious preferences of the negro remain close to the caterpillar and the cockroach. This is not stated to ridicule or abuse the negro. There is nothing fundamentally wrong with the caterpillar or the cockroach. It is merely a matter of taste. A cockroach or caterpillar remains proper food for a chimpanzee.

And the philosophic symbolism of black as connoting inferior intellect is implicit in the following passage: [6]

The way I look at it is this way: God didn't put the different races here to all mix and mingle so you wouldn't know them apart. He put them here as separate races and He meant for them to stay that way. I don't say He put the Caucasians here to rule the world or anything like that. I don't say He put them here to be the superior race; but since they have superior intellect and intelligences, I don't think God would want them to mingle with inferior races and lose their superiority. You know the Negro race is inferior mentally, everyone knows that, and I don't think God meant for a superior race like the Whites to blend with an inferior race and become mediocre.

In the above passages, one can see black as a negative philosophic symbol of being and truth. Black is ignorance, is lesser being. White, on the other hand, is a symbol of truth and of superior being. White people are the elect, endowed with superior intellects, who must flee contamination from darkness. Now, to correct this one-sided symbolism, it is necessary to trace it to its philosophic source.

As we noted earlier, the philosophic origin of the Western symbolism of color in which black is untruth and nonbeing while white is truth and being is traceable to the Christian followers of Plato's philosophy who took only the rational and logical side of Plato's philosophy. The mystical and allegorical writings of Plato were deemphasized and the root of Platonic philosophy in myth and religion was conveniently forgotten.

The Christians who used Platonic philosophy as a framework for their theological formulations considered *The Republic* of Plato his greatest writing. In this work is contained the famous allegory of the cave which may be considered to sum up the symbolism of light and darkness in Plato's philosophy. The cave represents this world which is dark; outside the cave is the bright light of the sun which represents the true and enduring world beyond this world, illumined by the beneficent rays of the Good. The dialectic in Plato is from darkness to light, that is, a departure from this present world into the other world beyond. This present world is the region of sin, error and mere opinion; the other world, in contrast, is the realm of truth and certainty, the real and the unchanging. The cave, too, represents the darkness of the human mind, ignorant and bereft of the knowledge of eternal forms, filled only with sense knowledge which furnishes one with mere opinion. The illuminated world outside the cave represents the state of the human mind illumined by the Divine Intellect and is therefore possessed of eternal forms. Darkness is thus equated with lack of awareness, with a state of unconsciousness, while light is equated with awareness and a state of consciousness.

The philosophic basis for the cave allegory is Plato's negative experience of time. Plato, Aristotle and Plotinus who represent the Apollonian strain of Greek thought saw time as negative rather than as positive. In other words, time as it moves forward into the future tends to death or nonbeing. For Plato, time is but a moving imitation of eternity.[7] The world as under the control and power of time is therefore just an image, not the reality. The real is outside time in another world. Hence, the world as image is a shadow and is seen darkly just as time is a shadow of eternity. Time in its forward movement into the future is not creative of reality. It is destructive rather than constructive and preservative. It descends rather than ascends.

Plotinus who followed his master Plato closely also saw time as negative. Time for Plotinus was a measure of the degradation or fall of the finite world from the One, that is, the Source of being.[8] As the world and all in it move farther into the future, there is a greater degradation and also greater darkness since one is farther away from the One who is Being and Light. The absolute future is thus to be expressed symbolically as nonbeing or pure nothingness and absolute darkness.

For Aristotle, too, time is seen as destructive rather than creative as it flows into the future. Thus, he says: "All change is by its nature an undoing. It is in time that all is engendered and destroyed. . . . One can see that time itself is the cause of destruction rather than generation. . . . For change itself is an undoing; it is only by accident a cause of generation and existence." [9] He expresses the same idea in a more philosophic way: "For we are wont to say that time wears, that all things age in time, all is erased by time, but never that we have learnt or that we have grown young and handsome; for time in itself is more truly a cause of destruction, since time is the number of movement, and movement undoes that which is." [10]

In accordance with the foregoing idea of time as negative or dark, Plato sought to escape the darkness of time into the light of the eternal and immutable, into the other-worldly region of Pure Forms. Aristotle, however, saw the doctrine of pure forms as superfluous and therefore tried to get rid of the other-worldly realm by incarnating the pure forms, so to speak, into this world, making them the essences or natures of things. The real is now to be sought in this world, not in the past by reminiscence as in Plato, nor in the future which is not yet, but in the present. In spite of this change, the negative philosophical symbolism of darkness did not change. Darkness as negative still symbolized the nonbeing of the past and the not-yet-being of the future; light, on the other hand, symbolized the present as the region of being and truth.

Even in the classical empirical phase of Western philosophy, that is, the age of Locke, Berkeley and Hume, the symbolism of light and darkness held. Like Aristotelian philosophy, the present was the place of being and truth, hence symbolized by light; the past and the future as nonbeing and therefore unknowable were symbolized by darkness. The difference between Aristotelian metaphysical philosophy and classical empiricism is in the conception of the real- and of truth-in-the-present. For Aristotle, the real is the existing essence or nature behind phenomena or appearance and truth or knowledge is to know what the essence and nature of a given thing is. For empiricism, there is no substance or essence or nature behind phenomena. There are only phenomena. To know is to know an impression or an idea, that is, a phenomenon.

From the point of view of process philosophy, however, both metaphysical and empirical philosophies are similar in locating being and truth in the present. The ultimate philosophic reason for locating being (ontological) and truth (epistemological) in the present is the negative view of time as nonevolutionary. If we were to illustrate diagrammatically the ontological structure of the real (being) based on this nonevolutionary view of time it would appear thus:

past [11]	present	future
nonbeing	being	nonbeing

In the above nonevolutionary view of time, only present time is real since the past and future being nonexistent are unreal. Accordingly, being or the real is located in the present. Since to have being is to have an essence or nature (Aristotle) or to have an appearance or a set of phenomena (empiricism) then truth as the objective possession of an essence or of a set of phenomena is likewise located in the present. Truth follows being. Where being is, there truth is also. Thus, diagrammatically, we have:

past	present	future
untruth	truth	untruth

Since the past and the future are nonbeing, there is nothing to be known, hence there is no truth to be found there. The knowing subject can know only being, not nonbeing. Since being and objective truth are located in the present, knowledge or consciousness as the presence of forms (essence or phenomenon) in the mind can take place only in the dimension of the present. In relation to the past and future, the conceptual mind (as opposed to memory and foresight) is unaware or is unknowing, hence, unconscious. Consciousness follows being and truth. Hence, diagrammatically, we have:

past	present	future
unconsciousness	consciousness	unconsciousness
or	or	or
lack of knowledge	knowledge	lack of knowledge

Having described the ontological and epistemological structures of what I might call Apollonian philosophy (as opposed to the Dionysian) let us now see how these ontological and epistemological structures may be symbolized in terms of light and darkness.

Consciousness is a light. We can see better this essential trait of consciousness if we use the term intellect whose derivation is from the term *lux* (light). The intellect is a seeing faculty. To have no intellect is to be blind, hence to be in darkness. By transference from the knowing faculty to the object known, truth itself which is the object of the intellect is called a light, while the absence of truth or ignorance is called darkness.

Because of the convertibility of truth and being, the latter is also symbolized as light while nonbeing is symbolized as darkness. Again, the symbolism of light and darkness ultimately is based on the nonevolutionary view of time. This view may be symbolized in terms of light and darkness thus:

past	present	future
darkness	light	darkness

In the diagram, we note that the present as the region of being, truth and consciousness is symbolized by light. In the present the intellect can see forms of objects. Just as we see forms of objects during the day because there is sunlight so we symbolize the present as the region of day or the region of the visible. The past and the future in contrast to the present are symbolized as the region of darkness because they are the region of nonbeing, of unconsciousness, of untruth. They are also symbolized as the region of night and of the invisible since the past and future are formless, that is, there are no forms of objects to be seen since the past and the future are in a state of nonbeing.

Let us illustrate in a diagram how the symbolism of light and darkness is applied in the Apollonian ontological and epistemological views of being and truth:

	past	present	future
ontological:	nonbeing	being	nonbeing
epistemological:	untruth	truth	untruth
	un-consciousness	consciousness	un-consciousness
symbolism:	darkness	light	darkness
	night	day	night
	invisible	visible	invisible

One can observe from the above schema that Apollonian philosophy is dualistic. In terms of symbolism, light is wholly positive, darkness wholly negative. Light is equated with being, truth, consciousness; darkness with nonbeing, untruth and an inferior level of consciousness. This Apollonian philosophic symbolism of light and darkness is the frame of reference and meaning for Apollonian white theology and is the implicit basis of modern Apollonian Western culture and language. Imbued and conditioned by this philosophy, Apollonian Western man's attitude toward darkness is one of flight, repulsion, hatred. If there is a darkness, a shadow, a cloud in our lives, we must flee from it, expel it. The ideal person is one in whom there is no darkness whatsoever. This means that he has the fullness of being, truth, and consciousness.

The Apollonian philosophic attitude toward darkness is reenforced and confirmed by Apollonian Christian theology. Thus, the philosophic struggle against darkness is endowed with a religious dimension and with a holy zeal. Darkness now means a struggle against sin and the Devil, for God is the Light in whom there is no darkness. The attainment of God who is symbolized as the Light is philosophically expressed as the attainment of Being, Truth and Goodness.

Because of the phenomenon of projection, which we noted in a previous chapter, the negative attitude toward darkness is projected into the outculture, in this case people with dark skins. One can see how the authority of philosophy and theology has given the Apollonian man a self-righteous attitude in his relation with dark-skinned peoples. We can see too how philosophic and theological racism are the root cause of economic racism. Because of this fact, even if the black man has obtained economic parity with the white man, he will still be considered inferior in the eyes of the white man because of philosophic and theological propositions that make white superior to black, light superior to darkness. Hence, there is need of counteracting racism at the philosophic and theological levels.

Let us then show a different philosophic frame of reference in which darkness is an ambivalent value. Now, just as the ultimate philosophic basis for Apollonian philosophy was the negative experience of time, so the starting point of the process philosophy we present here is time except that the experience of it is a positive one. The positive experience of time is based on our awareness of evolution. Evolution implies that time is creative of novelty, of new being, as it moves forward, such that there is more in the end than at the beginning. In other words, the movement of time forward is a process of maturation and development. Now we do not deny that Aristotle had a notion of development, in the sense of the maturation of an individual from an infant to the adult. But Aristotle did not have a notion of evolution in the sense that biological species evolve from previous ones. For him species were fixed, eternal, universal. Today, we are aware of a macrocosmic or overall process of evolution which includes all things in time. The things we see in the world like minerals, plants, animals, men did not come into being all at once or simultaneously but sequentially and in a definite order measured by complexity of organization. First there was the evolution of matter, then the evolution of life, next the evolution of consciousness. To put it another way, first there was matter that was both nonliving and non-thinking (the atom), then there evolved matter that was living but was nonthinking (the cell), and finally, there was matter that was both living and thinking (animals and men). This view of evolution shows time as positive, that is, as not merely preserving what was originally there in the begin-ning or destroying them as they tended toward the future, but as producing more being as time moves forward. With this view of time, we are now in a position to sketch a processive view of reality.[12]

A processive world-view would put being in the future, becoming in the present, and germinal being or "nonbeing" in the past. Being in the processive world-view is equated with maturity or fullness of development. For any given thing then that is in process of evolution, being is future. Of course, in a sense, being as meaning present existence is located only in the present because the past no longer exists and the future does not yet exist. But being in the sense of ability to survive or greater independence is not found in the existence of a presently developing thing, but in the state of maturity and fullness of development. Evolution shows that mortality is greatest or is most likely to occur at the early stages of development.

A deeper and more abstract reflection on the reality of the present will show that the present does not really have any independent existence apart from the past and the future. Whatever reality the present has is owed to the past from which it evolved and to the future toward which it will evolve. It is an illusion to think of the present as having an existence of its own. Shear off the future from the present and the present ceases to exist. The only way the present can endure is for it to move forward. If there were no future to move forward to, the present would stop. It would cease to exist. The future then is the true being of the present. It is also the region of fullness, of maturation. Hence, in the processive world-view, being is located in the future. The future does not mean the cessation of activity. When that which is becoming or growing reaches its fullness in that line of growth, it attains being, in that line of becoming. But the attainment of being precisely means the attainment of adulthood compared to the infant stage. Adulthood means the possession of the fullness of one's powers, hence, the fullness of activity. Let us diagram the ontological structure of a processive view of reality:

past	present	future
nonbeing or germinal undeveloped	becoming developing	being developed

Now, as being so truth, or as the ontology so the epistemology. So, we would have to locate truth also in the future. Perhaps a further reflection for this identification is necessary. We said that what is becoming is not yet being, that is, it has not yet attained the fullness of what it is. It is not yet fully evolved. But what is evolution but the differentiation of parts? In other words, what was merely there germinally, or hidden is now manifested or revealed in the process of differentiation or development. Thus, we see that the attainment of the fullness of being is also accompanied by the full manifestation of what a thing is. For example, the seed is revealed to be an oak. We thus see what a thing really is. Its truth or true form is manifested. Consequently, when a thing attains its fullness of being, it also attains its fullness of truth. It is revealed unto itself. Truth then is future just as being is. By way of contrast, the region of the present and of the past are the region of half-truth and untruth respectively. Let us explain what we mean. Since the present is the region of becoming, it means that the given thing is not yet fully differentiated, hence, not fully revealed. There is much of it that is yet concealed. We might say that it is half-revealed, half-concealed. Accordingly, as half-revealed, it is proper to describe it as half-true. Truth, we said earlier, follows being. So what is half-being (undeveloped, becoming) is only half-true. By comparison to the present, the past as the region of the germinal is relatively to be considered nonbeing, for it has not yet begun its process of becoming, much like a seed on the table which in the line of its own evolution has not started the process of its germination. Left on the table the seed shrivels up and dies. Because of this direction toward death it is proper to say that it is in a state of nonbeing. Again, as truth follows being, so, as the state of nonbeing of that which is not evolving, so it is untrue. The epistemological structure of evolving reality may be illustrated thus:

past	present	future
untruth	half-truth	fullness of truth
absence of truth	half-false	absence of falsehood

Let us now consider the ontological structure, that is, the reality of consciousness as process. Consciousness as a power of knowing develops and evolves like everything in evolutionary time. Its development is the process of growth of consciousness in a given individual while its evolution is the evolution of collective consciousness of which individual consciousness is a part. Whether individual or collective, consciousness has a stage of birth, a stage of becoming and a stage of maturation. Diagrammatically, we may illustrate the process of consciousness thus:

past	present	future
unconscious	half-conscious half-unconscious	fully conscious

In the above diagram we observe that consciousness evolves from unconsciousness to consciousness. The midpoint of its evolution is occupied by our present historical consciousness whose structure is that of a half-evolved reality, hence, it is half-conscious.

Having described what being, truth and consciousness are as processes, let us now see how they are symbolized in terms of light and darkness. Diagrammatically we have:

	past	present	future
ontological:	nonbeing	becoming	full being
epistemological:	untruth unconscious	half-truth half-conscious	full truth fully conscious
symbol:	darkness night invisible	half-light half-darkness night and day half-visible	light day full revelation

You will notice in the above diagram that light is located in the future, darkness in the past and the region of night and day in the present or in historical time. But a very important observation here is that though the future is symbolized as light, our present historical consciousness does not experience the future as light. Rather, it experiences it as darkness. The reason for this is that the ontological structure of present historical consciousness is a state of half-consciousness. This means that it has darkness within itself since it is not fully conscious. It projects this darkness outward. Thus the future is dark, for it transcends the power and capacity of present historical consciousness. Being half-conscious, it is not able to comprehend fully what being and truth are. The experience of darkness by present historical consciousness in relation to the future is like the experience of the eyes being blinded by too much light as when they look directly at the sun. It is the present that is experienced as light because our present consciousness is adequate for knowing objects in the present. The past is experienced as darkness for things in the dim past are lost sight of. Now this experience of present historical consciousness seems similar to the experience of Apollonian consciousness which also experiences the past and future as darkness and the present as light. But upon closer inspection, there is a great difference. To Apollonian consciousness the future is experienced as negative darkness because the future is nonbeing and is untrue, but to a processive consciousness, the darkness of the future is a positive darkness because it is the region of the fullness of being and of truth. Thus to processive consciousness, being and truth are symbolized as positive darkness. We may illustrate the epistemological structure of historical consciousness in terms of light and darkness thus:

past	present	future
negative darkness	light	positive darkness

Thus, from the point of view of consciousness-in-the-present, there are two levels of unknowing. The first is a negative unknowing or unconsciousness because it is based on what is germinal or undeveloped. There is nothing yet to be seen. But the other type of unconsciousness is really a higher dimension of consciousness or a superconsciousness toward which present consciousness is tending.

In the processive view of reality, to tend toward being and truth is to tend toward positive darkness. In the Apollonian static and nonevolutionary view of reality, darkness is wholly negative, consequently, one endeavors to flee it, to expel it from one's own being. The dialectic of fulfillment is for one to move from darkness to light. But in the processive view, the dialectic is from light to positive darkness, for what appears light does not always contain being and truth and what appears dark is not always an indication of nonbeing and absence of truth. Of course, the emotional reaction of the knower to darkness or to what is unknown or alien is fear and one flees from that which one fears. The fear of the child of the dark becomes in this case the fear of what is epistemologically dark or unknown. But the way to fulfillment in the processive world view is to embrace the dark as positive, as saving darkness, for the future as dark is the region of being and truth. There is risk involved, since darkness could also be negative. But to flee all darkness or all shadow from without and from within us is to be split, to be schizophrenic, and those who operate within the context in which darkness or shadow is wholly negative, be they white or black, are split in their beings, their egos. This split, in the case of whites is projected into the world outside as racism.

Modern psychology corroborates the processive world view of the shadow or darkness in us as not only negative but positive. In man there is the dimension of consciousness but also the dimension of what is called the Unconscious. It is the dark side of man, the shadow. This region as darkness is both negative and positive. It could destroy one but it could also heal one. Thus, as Erich Neumann observes, "the shadow is the 'guardian of the threshold', across which the path leads into the nether realm of transformation and renewal. And so what first appears to the ego as a devil becomes a psychopomp, a guide of the soul, who leads the way into the underworld of the unconscious—which however includes hell as well as the realm of the Mothers." [13] Thus, we see that the Unconscious, symbolized by the shadow, which is the dark side of man or of the soul is not only negative but also positive. It can be the source of death (hell) for the soul; it can be the source of life (transformation or rebirth). In either case, the shadow or darkness is the only path. It is, as Neumann notes, the guardian of the threshold.

In Apollonian symbolism, the shadow or darkness cannot be a source of integration, rebirth and transformation because it is seen wholly as negative, destructive of self. Selfhood is identified with consciousness (light, white). As Alan Watts notes, Western thought identifies wisdom with conscious reason instead of with the Unconscious.[14] Yet conscious reason is merely the surface of the psyche like the tip of an iceberg. Or to use another metaphor, the ground of reason is the unconscious. Apollonian thought defines man in terms of his conscious reason. He is defined as a rational animal. What is forgotten is that man is not yet rational. He is still very much irrational. Racism is a case in point. Man must achieve rationality, selfhood. But with the dualistic frame of reference which sees the unconscious as the opposite and enemy of the conscious, Western man has been fleeing from the true man. Western logic is static logic, the logic of Aristotle based on the principle of noncontradiction, namely, that the truth of A is in A, or A is A and could not also be non-A. Following this logic, the truth of conscious reason (represented by white culture and values) is in maintaining itself by fleeing from the realm of the unconscious seen as darkness (sin, evil, myth, etc.). It could not see by its logic that the truth of A is non-A, that is, that what appears to it as foreign, alien and negative is really in and for itself really positive—the truth of A.

To conclude this chapter we note that darkness or blackness at the philosophic and psychological levels is not a negative symbol only but also a positive one—the symbol of being and truth. In psychological terms, darkness is a symbol of the unconscious which, however, is ambivalent. In process thought, the region of the positive unconscious coincides with the absolute future, for, as we noted earlier, the future is experienced by present historical consciousness as a positive darkness, positive in that it is the source of its maturation and fulfillment, darkness in that the form and shape of this maturation is still unknown.

In the light of the philosophy of process in which darkness has been shown to be an ambivalent value as opposed to the Aristotelian one in which darkness is a negative value only, we are now in a position to examine the scriptures for the ambivalent symbolism of darkness.

8

BLACK AS A POSITIVE
CHRISTIAN SYMBOL

In the previous chapter, we set the philosophic framework, that of a philosophy of process, whose logic is that of paradox, as the true frame of reference which will truly open our eyes to the true symbolism of color found in the scriptures. We maintain that because the Apollonian mind viewed the scriptures with Aristotelian spectacles, it failed to see the paradoxical symbolism of the color black. In accordance with Aristotelian logic, the Apollonian mind reasoned that if black is negative in symbolism, which seems to be the case based on the great number of passages in which the color black and its correlative terms are used in a negative sense, then it could not also symbolize the positive. Accordingly, it explained away the positive symbolism as an exception.[1]

As an aid to understanding the use of black as a positive symbol in the passages to be examined, the processive frame of reference outlined previously should be kept before our minds. Let us repeat the diagram here:

α	β	Ω
negative darkness	light	positive darkness

In the diagram, point α (alpha) represents nonbeing, untruth, hence, negative darkness; point Ω (omega) represents being and truth, hence positive darkness. It is at omega that Yahweh is situated for that is the region of the supremely real; there, too, revelation and faith as the fullness of truth are situated. In accordance with the above frame of reference, the proper symbol for Yahweh is darkness; he dwells in darkness; his abode is in the clouds, that is, hidden from view. God is a *deus absconditus,* that is, a hidden God. Therefore, if he dwells in darkness, the time for his revelation is at night, in dreams. Revelation and Faith are also symbolized as darkness for they transcend the power of present historical consciousness.

The diagram will also help us to understand the negative use of black or darkness as a symbol. We recall in a previous chapter that black or darkness is used to symbolize sin, misfortune, the devil, hell, lack of faith and of truth, the absence of God and so on. Thus, in terms of the schema, we can place all these negative theological categories on the left side, that is, at point alpha which is symbolized by negative darkness.

In the Apollonian-Aristotelian schema of white theology there are only two columns, one for darkness which is negative and the other for light which is positive. Therefore there is no place to put those scriptural passages in which darkness is used as a positive symbol. To save the schema, these passages are conveniently ignored.

Let us now proceed to examine darkness as a positive symbol. First let us consider the symbolism of night. Recall what we noted in an earlier chapter of the negative symbolism of night. Night was a plague that punished the Egyptians; night was a symbol of moral evil as in the night of the soul; night is the symbol of Satan who plots his evil plans in the dark; night is the symbol of death, of Hades; night was the time Christ was betrayed, and so on.

But night, paradoxically, is also the symbol of the presence of God and the time of his communications; it is the time chosen for redemption, and in a more profound sense, night is a saving darkness.

The following passages show the association of night and God's presence in dreams and apparitions: [2]

If any man among you is a prophet
I make myself known to him in a vision,
I speak to him in a dream.   Num. 12:6.

God visited Abimelech in a dream at night . . .
Gen. 20:3.

At Gibeon Yahweh appeared in a dream to Solomon
during the night . . .   3 Kings 3:5.

That very night the word of Yahweh came to Nathan.
2 Kings 7:4.

God came to Balaam during the night and said to him . . .
Num. 22:20.

God came by night in a dream to Laban the Aramean . . .   Gen. 31:24.

We might note here the similarity between the mode of communication of the Israelite and his God, Yahweh, through dreams and the mode of communication of the native mind in other cultures with the numinous through dreams. The frequency of this mode of divine communication suggests more than an accidental connection. To an Apollonian mind the association of nighttime and God's presence is considered an exception for in his a priori view God is light, hence he is associated with the daytime not with the night. We shall put off till the next chapter a theological explanation for the positive connection between night and the divine presence. Suffice it to note here that in the scriptures night is positively associated with God's presence and his communications.

Nighttime is also associated with creativity, birth of new life and new being at both the physical and spiritual levels. Thus, it is during the night that life was conceived:

> This very evening, I [Raphael] promise, she will be given you as your wife. Then once you are in the bridal room, take the heart and liver of the fish and lay a little of it on the burning incense. . . . Then, before you sleep together, first stand up, both of you and pray. Ask the Lord of heaven to grant you his grace and protection. Do not be afraid; she was destined for you from the beginning, and it is you who will save her. She will follow you, and I will pledge my word, she will give you children who will be like brothers to you.
>
> Tobit 6:16-18.

At the spiritual level, night was the time of redemption. Redemption in the wide sense of the term means the preservation and continuation of life by buying it back. In this wide sense night is the appropriate time:

> In the middle of the night the man started up and looked about him; and there lying at his feet was a woman. "Who are you?" he said; and she replied, "I am Ruth, your maidservant. Spread the skirt of your cloak over your servant for you have the right of redemption over me."
>
> Ruth 3:8-9.

From the modern mind's point of view, the two passages just

cited do not seem to show any special theological significance to night as the time of redemption. And even at the secular level, night does not seem to have any special significance aside from the fact that it is at night that sexual union is normally performed. For the Israelites, however, there is no distinction between the religious and the secular, the supernatural and the natural. All of created reality and all of life are religious or supernatural. God is active in a supernatural way in all areas of created reality. Therefore the above passages are to be seen in the larger context of God's redemptive plan. Within this larger context there is a positive meaning to evening or to night that is largely supernatural, hence acts associated with nighttime have religious meaning.

Let us consider the larger context of God's redemptive plan in which night has a special significance and symbolism. In the strict sense of redemption as salvation from death and from sin, night is the time of its occurrence:

> That night, the flesh is to be eaten, roasted over the fire; it must be eaten with unleavened bread and bitter herbs. Do not eat any of it raw or boiled, but roasted over the fire, head, feet and entrails. You must not leave any over till the morning; whatever is left till morning you are to burn. You shall eat it like this: with a girdle round your waist, sandals on your feet, a staff in your hand. You shall eat it hastily: it is a passover in honour of Yahweh. That night, I will go through the land of Egypt and strike down all the first-born in the land of Egypt, man and beast alike, and I shall deal out punishment to all the gods of Egypt, I am Yahweh!
>
> Ex. 11:8-13.

The Passover was the highpoint of the Israelite's consciousness of Yahweh's redemptive action. It was this act of de-

liverance which gave fuller meaning to previous acts of de-
liverance and redemption. In the Passover there was a
definite association between night and redemption. Night was
an ambivalent symbol. It was a blessed night for the Israelite;
an accursed night for the Egyptians. The significance and
symbolism of night here gave fuller meaning to night in the
context of redemption taken in the wider sense.

The Passover was also seen by the Israelite as the fullness
and fulfillment of the first divine act of creation in which
darkness hovered over the deep.[4] Consequently, he saw the
night of the Passover as the fulfillment and recapitulation
of the "night" of the first creation.

Let us cite the passage in Genesis which relates the first
act of creation:

> In the beginning God created the heavens and the
> earth. Now the earth was a formless void, there was
> darkness over the deep, and God's spirit hovered over
> the water.
>
> God said, "Let there be light," and there was light.
> God saw that light was good, and God divided light
> from darkness. God called light "day," and darkness he
> called "night." Gen. 1:1-5.

Contrary to the popular theological view that darkness in
the above account was exclusively the symbol of evil or of
chaos (formlessness), the Genesis account sees darkness as
ambivalent. There is the positive darkness that hovered over
the deep, symbolic of the darkness of the watery womb. The
imagery used to portray the act of creation is human conception and birth. Just as in human conception, the watery
womb is vivified, given life or spirit, so God's spirit hovers
over the watery deep enveloped in darkness. Darkness in this
case is a necessary condition for conception or creativity,

hence positive.[5] It precedes that which is created—light. Opposed to light is darkness which in this case is negative, for it is opposed to creativity. There is thus a positive and a negative darkness.

The Israelites saw the divine darkness that hovered over the deep as the same darkness that was salvific, liberating them from bondage and creating of them a new and chosen people. Traditional theology is unable to see the continuity between the first act of creation and the redemptive act of the Passover, for it sees creation as a natural act while the Passover event was a redemptive (soteriological) act.[6] For this reason it is unable to see the significance of the symbolism of night or darkness. But for the Israelites the first act of creation was redemptive. As Stanley notes: [7]

> The view of Deutero-Isaias is that Yahweh will work Israel's definitive salvation as creator (Is 43:18-19; 48:6ff; cf. also Is 65:17ff.), for the reason that God's creation of the universe is thought of as pertaining to the same theological category as His covenant (Is 52:15-16; cf. also Is 66:22). This conception of the creation as a saving event is, I believe, the basis of the biblical view that the *eschaton* must correspond to the beginning, that eschatology, in other words, is determined by protology or ktisiology.

The reason for the continuity between the first act of creation and the Passover is due to the similarity of symbolism. For example, the waters of the Red Sea that saved the Israelites point to the waters of the first creation that brought forth life and being. As the watery deep was the dark womb from which created reality was born, so the dark waters of the Red Sea was the womb from which the new-born people emerged. And as the universal darkness was creative of new being, so the night of the Passover was creative, and vice versa, as the Passover night was redemptive, so the darkness of the first creation. Just as the symbolism of night of the first creation was associated with sexual images (the Spirit fecundating the waters symbolizing the union of the Infinite with the finite), so the night of the Passover symbolized the covenant union of Yahweh and the fleeing Israelites resulting in the birth of a new people from the watery depth of the Red Sea.[8]

It was not only the events of dreams, of the first creation, of the Passover and other accounts such as that of Ruth meeting Boaz at night that gave to the Israelites the consciousness of night as positive, signifying the divine presence, but also the fact that Yahweh himself is associated with darkness. Thus, in the following passage, darkness itself is the secret place of Yahweh:

> He bent the heavens and came down,
> a dark cloud under his feet;
> he mounted a cherub and flew,
> and soared on the wings of the wind.
>
> Darkness he made a veil to surround him,
> his tent a watery darkness, a dense cloud;
> before him a flash enkindled
> hail and fiery embers.   Ps. 18:9-12.

Note in the foregoing passage that Yahweh's tent is a watery darkness. This imagery seems to point to the watery darkness of the first creation and the watery darkness of the sea through which the Israelites crossed.

The experience of the Israelites of Yahweh, their God, is expressed in the imagery of darkness and clouds. Thus:

Moses answered the people, "Do not be afraid; God has

come to test you, so that your fear of him, being always in your mind, may keep you from sinning." So the people kept their distance while Moses approached the dark cloud where God was. Ex. 20:20-21.

Again, we have the following:

> Now when the priests came out of the sanctuary, the cloud filled the Temple of Yahweh, and because of the cloud the priests could no longer perform their duties: the glory of Yahweh filled Yahweh's Temple.
> Then Solomon said:
> Yahweh has chosen to dwell in the thick cloud.
> Yes, I have built you a dwelling,
> a place for you to live for ever. 1 Kings 8:10-13.

> Yahweh is king! Let earth rejoice.
> the many isles be glad!
> Cloud and Darkness surround him,
> Righteousness and Justice support his throne.
> Ps. 97:1-2.

Thus, darkness is spoken of as encompassing the presence of God, as that out of which he speaks—the envelope, as it were, of divine glory.

For the Israelites, then, since darkness was symbolic of the divine presence itself, night was the appropriate time for his communications and his saving acts. The view of night as a positive symbol is had not only by the Old Testament but also by the New Testament. Thus, the night of the first creation and the night of the Passover are continued in the night of Mary's visitation. With Mary's fiat, the Holy Spirit —that same Spirit that hovered over the dark waters in the first creation, fecundating it—now fecundates the dark waters of Mary's womb. There results a new creation, a new being, who is the definitive source of redemption and salvation. In Christ is a new covenant which continues and fulfills the first covenant of creation and the Mosaic covenant.

Christ is a new creation, in the same line as the first creation and the creation of the Israelite people.[9] Now, just as creativity in the Old Testament was associated with darkness, with night, so the coming of Christ took place at night —in Bethlehem, in the middle of the night, Christ came silently into the world. The blessed night of the Passover is fulfilled in the holy night of the Incarnation.

The coming of Christ does not finish the redemptive process. Christ had a work to do. This redemptive work which was an act of creation—the creation of a new Qahal Yahweh (new Church) was finally accomplished at night— the night of the Last Supper, but also the night of Jesus' arrest and betrayal. Thus, the ambivalence of darkness or night in the creation and Passover events is repeated here in the new Passover. It was not accidental that Christ chose the time of night for the final redemptive act. Night was the symbol of creativity, it was the time of union exemplified most of all by sexual union. Christ's redemptive act was a new creation and this new creation was a spiritual union between God and man guaranteed by the formation of the New Covenant.

Night is not merely a temporary symbol of creativity and redemption. It is a permanent symbol of the end or of the eschaton. Thus, from an eschatological perspective, the last judgment, at once a calamity and a victory will occur at night:[10]

I tell you, on that night two will be in one bed: one will be taken, the other left; two women will be grinding corn together: one will be taken, the other left.

Luke 17:34-35.

Again we have the following passage:

> Then the kingdom of heaven will be like this: Ten
> bridesmaids took their lamps and went to meet the
> bridegroom. Five of them were foolish and five were
> sensible: the foolish ones did take their lamps, but they
> brought no oil, whereas the sensible ones took flasks of
> oil as well as their lamps. The bridegroom was late, and
> they all grew drowsy and fell asleep. But at midnight
> there was a cry, "The bridegroom is here! Go out and
> meet him."   Mt. 25:1-7.

As we noted earlier, the eschaton corresponds to the beginning, hence, the night of the first creation corresponds to the
night of the new creation. For the Christian, the night of the
first creation is fulfilled in the night of the resurrection of
Jesus from the darkness of the tomb. The Christian celebrates
Christ's death and resurrection as he was commanded to do
by Christ himself. Just as the Jew celebrates the memory of
the Passover, so the Christian celebrates Christ's Passover.
He performs the celebration at night and he sees this night
as the same night of Christ's resurrection, Last Supper, incarnation and as the same night of the first Passover.

Permit us to quote at length from the Christian Liturgy
to show the positive symbolism of night. Thus, in the liturgy
for Holy Saturday, all the past events leading to the blessed
night of Christ's Last Supper are remembered and shown to
point to this final event as to their fullness and fulfillment:

> For this is the Paschal solemnity, in which that true
> Lamb is slain, by whose blood the doorposts of the
> faithful are hallowed. This is the night in which Thou
> didst first cause our forefathers, the children of Egypt,
> to pass through the Red Sea with dry feet. This, there-
> fore, is the night which purged away the darkness of

sinners by the light of the pillar. This is the night which
at this time throughout the world restores to grace and
unites in sanctity those that believe in Christ, and are
separated from the vices of the world and the darkness
of sinners. This is the night in which, destroying the
bonds of death, Christ arose victorious from the grave.
. . . O truly blessed night, which alone deserved to
know the time and hour in which Christ rose again from
the grave! This is the night of which it is written: And
the night shall be enlightened as the day; and the night
is my light in my enjoyments. Therefore the holiness of
this night drives away all wickedness, cleanses faults
and restores innocence to the fallen, and gladness to the
sorrowful. It puts to flight hatred, brings peace and
humbles pride.

O truly blessed night, which despoiled the Egyptians
and enriched the Hebrews! A night in which heavenly
things are united to those of earth, and things divine
to those which are human. . . .

Notice in the above passage the ambivalent symbolism of
night. It is night in the positive sense that drives away the
darkness of sinners. Notice too the belief of Christians that
there is a continuity between the night of the Easter Vigil
today and the night of Christ's passion and resurrection, the
night of the flight from Egypt and the night of the desert
in the Exodus. There is an identification, as a matter of fact,
between "this night," that is, as celebrated today, and "those
nights" in the past salvific history. Those nights are not just
being remembered or memorialized, they are sacramentally
present. The salvific acts of those nights are repeated, reenacted this very night and are producing the same effects
on the chosen people today as they did to the Israelites and
to the followers of Jesus during his day. Hence, night or

darkness is a permanent and abiding symbol of Christianity. The liturgical year tends toward and is centered upon the sacred and blessed night of the Easter Vigil. That night is our salvation, is our light, as the Holy Saturday preface reminds us. It is our hope of restoration from sin, the time when God is present, hence our hope of rebirth.

It is the belief of Christians that the salvific acts done to the collective are reenacted and recapitulated in the life of the individual. Thus baptism and the act of faith are a reenactment of the first creation, of the creation of Israel as a new people, of the creation of the Church at the night of the Last Supper, of the new creation which is the new Adam, Christ, at the night of Jesus' resurrection, for baptism and faith are in themselves a new creation (Gal. 6:15; 2 Cor. 5:17). Hence, in the early Church liturgy, catechumens were baptized during the sacred night of the Easter Vigil and Christians renewed their faith and their baptismal vows.

Because of the continuity of baptism and faith with the salvific acts of God in both the Old and New Testaments, there is also a continuity of symbolism. Hence the darkness of baptism and of faith is the same as the darkness over the watery deep of the first creation, as the night of the Exodus when the Israelites went down to the dark waters of the sea, as the night of the Last Supper and the night of the resurrection of Jesus. Baptism is a going down to the watery darkness and coming forth a new being, a new Adam. The imagery used by none other than Christ himself is a being reborn, hence a going back to the darkness of the womb in a spiritual sense.[11]

Faith itself is a saving darkness, for we do not see. As Paul says, faith comes by hearing, not by sight (Rom. 10:17); and blessed are those that have not seen, and yet have believed (John 20:29). Again, Paul says we walk by faith, not by sight (2 Cor. 5:7), and faith is the substance of things hoped for, the evidence of things not seen (Heb. 11:1). Just as the Israelites had to have faith, trusting in the guidance of God through the night of the Exodus and the wanderings in the desert, so the Christian has to have faith for the Christian life is one long Exodus. It is a night of faith, but this night is salvific, hence, positive.

So far we have been discussing the positive symbolism of night and darkness and we have found that they are a pervading and primary symbol of the Old and New Testaments and of the Christian life as expressed in the Christian liturgy. Apollonian theology we might note has not sought to explain this pervading and positive symbolism of night and darkness. Instead it has used darkness or night as a wholly negative symbolism, hence unfaithful to its sources in the scriptures and the liturgy which are the norm of faith.

Let us devote the remainder of the chapter to discussing some correlative terms of darkness and night to show their ambivalence. Let us take first the notion of cloud in association with the divine presence. In Apollonian theology, dark clouds are a sign of evil, misfortune and divine disfavor. God himself is symbolized as Light in whom there is no cloud and the ideal Christian life is one that is cloudless in the sense that there is no darkness of sin in one's life. The Apollonian mind's preconception of God's manifestation is that of a superbrilliance that drives away all darkness. The imagery appropriate for God is that of a divine sun shining in a cloudless day.

A reexamination of the scriptures gives us another picture and imagery of God's manifestation.[12] As we noted earlier, God is said to dwell in darkness and when he reveals himself, he does so in a cloud.[13] Thus in the well-known revelation of God on Sinai it is said:

The cloud covered the mountain, and the glory of

Yahweh settled on the mountain of Sinai; for six days the cloud covered it, and on the seventh day Yahweh called to Moses from inside the cloud.   Ex. 24:16-17.

Again, the presence of Yahweh with the Israelites as they crossed the desert was in the form of a pillar of cloud:

Yahweh went before them, by day in the form of a pillar of cloud to show them the way, and by night in the form of a pillar of fire to give them light.   Ex. 13:21.

At the time of the dedication of the temple of Solomon the glory of Yahweh took the form of a cloud (3 Kings 8:11-12; 2 Par. 5:14); and Yahweh's tent was a dense cloud (Ps. 18:11). This symbol of the divine presence is now transferred to symbolize also his love:

This love of yours is like a morning cloud
Hos. 6:4.

The symbolism of the divine manifestation by clouds is not an isolated occurrence in the scriptures. As Maertens notes, "The cloud was a theme customary in the theophanies." [14] The cloud, a sign of divine presence rested upon Mary, the new Jerusalem (Lk. 1:35).

Just as night was the time for final or eschatological victory, so the cloud was an apocalyptic sign of salvation. It was a sign of Christ's return: [15]

As he said this he was lifted up while they looked on, and a cloud took him from their sight. They were still staring into the sky when suddenly two men in white were standing near them and they said, "Why are you men from Galilee standing here looking into the sky?

Jesus who has been taken up from you into heaven, this
same Jesus will come back in the same way as you have
seen him go there."   Acts 1:9-11.

The foregoing passage seems to point back to an apocalyptic
passage in the Old Testament:

> I gazed into the visions of night
> and I saw, coming on the clouds of heaven,
> one like a son of man.   Dan. 7:13.

Another symbol closely associated with clouds is that of
the shadow or shade. Clouds provided shade, a symbol of
divine protection and closeness to God.[16] For example we
have the following passage:

> He was still speaking when suddenly a bright cloud
> covered them with shadow, and from the cloud there
> came a voice which said, "This is my Son, the Beloved;
> he enjoys my favour. Listen to him."   Matt. 17:5.

Negatively, the term shadow in the scriptures stands for
transitoriness and for the unreality of man's life, hence, life
as a shadow. And Psalm 23 speaks of "the valley of the
shadow of death." But the negative symbolism of shadow has
been overemphasized to the exclusion of the positive aspect
of shadow in the scriptures. As Maertens observes, the shadow
is an image to express the special protection of God over
his people.[17] Thus, just as one rests under a tree to recover
one's strength and to seek shelter from the oppressive heat
of the sun's rays, so the presence of God is considered to
give a sacred "Shade" and we rest secure under the shadow
of God. Maertens adds that it is in this sense that the shadow

of the Lord Jesus Christ in the New Testament was sufficient to heal the sick.[18]

Maertens shows the various positive symbolisms of shadow in the following passages: The restful shade of trees (Mark 4:32; Job 12:2; 3 Kings 19:5; Jonas 4:5-6); this shadow is a gift of the gods whom men adored near trees (Os. 4:13). Royal persons, compared to trees, were thought to give shade to their people, that is, security and protection (Judges 9:15; Ezech. 31:2-16; Isa. 30:2-3; Lam. 4:20). Similarly, Israel is a people who, growing like a tree, will shelter all nations under its shadow (Ps. 79:11; Os. 14:8; Ezech. 17:23). It was God who took it upon himself to give the shadow of his protection to Israel. This shadow came from the cloud which rested over the place where God's presence was found (Ex. 19:9-18; Wisd. 19:7; Isa. 4:5-6; 49:2; Ps. 16:8; 90:1; 120:5). The shadow of the new cloud, which is Christ, is in turn the place of divine protection for his people and the instrument of its healing (Mark 5:25-35; Acts 5:15; 19:11). The shadow consecrates by its presence the elect of God, Mary and the transfigured Christ, as if to show the special protection which they deserve because of their election (Luke 1:35; 9:34).

The shadow which is a symbol of divine protection is imaged not only by trees and clouds but also by wings. Thus, "Hide me under the shadow of thy wings" (Ps. 17:8); "Because thou has been my help, therefore in the shadow of thy wings will I rejoice" (Ps. 63:7); "He that dwelleth in the secret place of the most High shall abide under the shadow of the Almighty" (Ps. 91:1).

Finally, let us consider the symbols of black and white in the scriptures. Already we showed the negative symbolism of black, namely, that it symbolizes sin, damnation, hell, suffering, punishment, etc., and the positive symbolism of white, namely, as a symbol of purity, sinlessness, grace, glory, etc. Now, let us show the reverse symbolism.

Whiteness is also used in the scriptures to symbolize sin and punishment for sin. For example in the account of Naaman, the army commander to the king of Aram, who was cured of his leprosy by the prophet Elisha, the servant of the prophet named Gehazi, smitten by avarice decided to get for himself the gift from Naaman to Elisha which the prophet refused to accept. For this sin Gehazi was punished. Elisha pronounced the sentence of God upon him thus:

> "Naaman's leprosy will cling to you and to your descendants for ever." And Gehazi left his presence a leper, white as snow.   2 Kings 5:27.

In the scriptures, leprosy which is a whiteness of skin was a biblical sign of uncleanness and of sin (Lev. 13:8; 14:2; cf. also 2 Kings 5:6; 2 Chron. 26:21). It was a sign of divine displeasure, punishment, damnation. Christ's miracles and divine healing were especially demonstrated in the curing of lepers (Mk. 1:40; Lk. 7:22, 17:12; 5:13; 4:27; Mt. 8:3; 10:8; 11:5).

Another Old Testament account of whitness of skin as a sign of punishment is given in Numbers. There, Miriam and Aaron reproached Moses for marrying a Cushite woman, an event which however was blessed by Yahweh. Miriam's punishment is related thus:

> Suddenly, Yahweh said to Moses and Aaron and Miriam, "Come, all three of you, to the Tent of Meeting." They went, all three of them, and Yahweh came down in a pillar of cloud and stood at the entrance of the Tent. He called Aaron and Miriam and they both came forward. . . . How then have you dared to speak

against my servant Moses? . . . The anger of Yahweh blazed out against them. He departed, and as soon as the cloud withdrew from the Tent, there was Miriam a leper, white as snow! Aaron turned to look at her; she had become a leper.   Numbers 12:4-10.

It is in the context of the whiteness of skin taken as a negative symbol of punishment that we ought to interpret the passage in the Song of Songs in which the beauty of the bride is described as black and lovely (1:5). However, a different reading of the passage equates blackness of skin with a serious ordeal.[19] But whatever be the reading, it does not offset the fact that whiteness in the scriptures is not always a positive symbol.

We have shown sufficiently, we hope, that black and its correlative terms, night, darkness, shadow, cloud, are used not only as negative symbols but also as positive ones. Now, on the question as to which is the primary symbol of the positive, white or black, light or darkness, we answer that the question is a false one for it starts from the Aristotelian frame of reference that a term could have only one primary signification. All other meanings are secondary or metaphorical. With this a priori condition, white theology fixed the primary symbolism of black as negative and of white as positive. This position is supposedly supported by the greater number of passages in which white is used as a positive symbol rather than as a negative one and the greater number of passages in which black is used as a negative symbol compared to those in which it is used as a positive one.

A quantitative and statistical comparison of passages ignores the true basis of symbolism, namely, the degree of reality of that which is symbolized. We have shown that night and darkness symbolize the Supreme Reality, Yahweh. In the consciousness of both the Old Testament and the New Testament writers and of the early Christians as manifested in their liturgy, night and darkness are pervading and primary symbols of the central event of the Judeo-Christian religion, namely, the Passover. Unfortunately, Apollonian theology has not reflected this universal consciousness and experience of night or darkness as a positive and primary symbol. Hence our task now is to show how night or darkness could be a positive theological symbol.

9

A PROCESSIVE THEOLOGY
OF DARKNESS

In the previous chapter we came up with the evidence to show the positive symbolism of night as the time of the divine presence, of darkness as the symbol of the abode of God, of dark clouds as a manifestation of God's hiddenness, of the shadow as a sign of divine protection and of blackness as a sign of beauty. If we put these symbolisms side by side with the symbolisms in which night is equated with sin, darkness with the abode of the Devil, bright sky with happiness and whiteness with purity and divine favor, we come up with the impression that the scriptures are full of contradictions. But to one who believes the scriptures to be the revelation of the word of God there could be no contradictions; consequently an attempt is made to explain the apparent contradictions. The method of Apollonian theology, influenced by the epistemological notion of truth as the absence of contradiction, is to explain away one set of symbolism as an exception and the other as the rule. Thus, for example, a respected theologian tried to explain away the apparent contradiction in the symbolism of God as dwelling in darkness, on the one hand, and as dwelling in light, on the other, by considering the former as an exception. Thus, he writes: [1]

> It is an exception when Yahweh is said to set His dwelling in darkness (2 S 22:12; 1K 8:12; Ps 18:12). Here we have an allusion to the clouds of the storm theophany; Yahweh must veil His light when He appears, for no man can look upon it and live.

Let us quote here the passages from the scriptures which were cited above:

> Darkness he made a veil to surround him,
> his tent a watery darkness, dense cloud.
> > 2 Sam. 22:12.

> Yahweh has chosen to dwell in the thick cloud.
> > 1 Kings 8:12.

> Darkness he made a veil to surround him,
> his tent a watery darkness, dense cloud.
> > Ps. 18:12.

Now, let us compare the passages just quoted with the following:

> God is light, and in him is no darkness at all.
> > 1 Jn. 1:5ff.

And describing the heavenly city, the new Jerusalem, we have the following passage:

> There shall be night no more; and they need no lamp of night, neither light of sun, for the Lord God shall give them light.   Rev. 22:5.

Apollonian theology following Aristotelian logic reserves the symbolism of darkness for Satan and for Hades. Therefore the same symbol cannot also be applied to God and to the heavenly city. But as a matter of fact we find the scriptures using darkness as a symbol for the divine presence, for his abode, and if God's abode is heaven, then it too is symbolized as darkness—a watery darkness. What to do? The easy way out is to say that the symbolism of darkness is an exception. But this explanation is unsatisfactory. As long as we take this route by way of explanation, then why should the symbolism of darkness be the exception and not rather the symbolism of light? Is not the reason for this a priori choice the a priori negative attitude toward darkness? But what is the basis for this a priori negative attitude? It is not ordinary experience for we have shown that our experience of darkness and light is ambivalent. The basis could only be cultural and philosophic. The Apollonian mentality and philosophy were imposed upon the scriptures. This frame of reference conditioned and influenced one to ignore those passages in which darkness, night, shadow and blackness were used as positive symbols.

There would be sufficient reason to claim that the symbolism of darkness applied to God and to his abode is the exception if the use was an isolated case involving one or two passages. But we have shown in the previous chapter that the symbolism of night and darkness as positive runs through the whole of scripture, from Genesis to the Apocalypse. We showed that the symbolism of darkness and of night is not an exception in the minds of the Old Testament and New Testament writers nor to the early Christians as manifested in their liturgy. Night and darkness are the primary and appropriate symbols for redemption as a creative process. Hence, it is the primary symbol at the first creation, at the first Passover, at Christ's Passover, at the resurrection of

Jesus and even at the eschatological banquet. The Passover, the central event in the Judeo-Christian religion is a celebration of night—a night that is sacred and blessed for it destroys the darkness of sin, a night that unites earth with heaven and the human with the divine.

The description of God as dwelling in darkness is not an exception but is the normal experience of the Israelites whenever Yahweh decides to manifest himself to them. The uniqueness of Yahweh over other gods is his hiddenness. Yahweh is a *deus absconditus*. In the theophany on Sinai, Yahweh said to Moses: "I am coming to you in a dense cloud so that the people may hear when I speak to you" (Ex. 19:9, 16). Note in the words of Yahweh the manner of his revelation, namely, by hearing, not by sight. The aural takes priority over the visual since Yahweh is not seen. In Deuteronomy is stated: "Things hidden belong to Yahweh our God" in contrast to things seen which belong to the children of men (Deut. 29:28). In Apollonian philosophy and theology, the visual takes priority over the aural. In this frame of reference, light is the primary symbol and darkness as a mode of knowing would be an exception if not a contradiction. But in the aural frame of reference, darkness is the primary symbol.

If the symbols of night and darkness are pervading symbols of the scriptures and of the Judeo-Christian experience then it would be an inadequate theology which ignores or distorts or explains away the symbolisms. It is incumbent then upon us to attempt a theology in which darkness and night are presented and explained as central symbols of the Faith.

The theology of darkness we attempt to present here is based on a philosophy of process. We feel that this philosophy is not foreign to the scriptures for the scriptures present us with a process of redemption starting with the first creation and having as intermediate stages the first Passover, the second Passover of Christ, and as the final stage, the eschatological Passover which is the new creation. The redemptive process is a succession of rebirths in which transformation takes place from the old Adam to the new Adam, from the first creation to the new creation, from the old Jerusalem to the new Jerusalem and so on. You will observe in the process of transformation from the old to the new that there is a growth, a fullness of being and of truth at the end of the process of rebirth. We are justified then in presenting this process of transformation graphically thus:

α	β	Ω
old Adam		new Adam
old Jerusalem		new Jerusalem
old being (nonbeing)	becoming	new being

In the diagram above, the omega point which is the stage of the new Adam implies the stage of the fullness of being and of consciousness. It is the new Adam endowed with the fullness of being and of consciousness that is the judge of the old and of the intermediate stages before it, hence of the stage beta. The new Adam which is a new creation is still up ahead in the future. This future is not a historical future such as the year 3000, for example, but is the eschatological future, hence a totally new time dimension that transcends the historical time dimension.[2] That future is described scripturally as "the last times," the end of the world, the ushering in of the Kingdom.

Christ has gone ahead, the first fruit and the first born of those reborn to the Spirit. He is the new Adam. By becoming like him in his life and sufferings we too will rise with him, we too will be created anew into the new Adam. Scripturally, the process of transformation into the new Adam is described as a "rebirth" (Matt. 19:28; Jn. 3:3ff; Eph.

2:4-6; 1 John *passim;* 1 Pt. 1:3, 23; 2:2, etc.). But at present we are a pilgrim people, dwelling in tents like the wandering Israelites on their way to the Holy Land. There in the eschatological future we shall meet Yahweh.

In the scriptural frame of reference, Yahweh is situated at the omega point, at the eschatological future. As Jürgen Moltmann observes, in the Old Testament statements about the revealing God are combined throughout with statements about the promise of God. God reveals himself in the form of promise. And in the New Testament, God is known and described as the "God of promise" (Heb. 10:23; 11:11) and God of hope (Rom. 15:13). Thus Yahweh is a God with the eschatological future as his essential nature as made known in Exodus and in Israelite prophecy.[3] And Johann-Baptist Metz adds that Yahweh is a "God before us." [4]

Having given the scriptural frame of reference for the process of redemption we are now in a position to explain the scriptural symbolisms of God as dwelling in darkness, as a hidden God, as veiling himself in a cloud, of faith and revelation as darkness, of redemption as a going back to the dark waters of the womb and so on.

Recall again what we said above that we are a pilgrim people going to the Holy Land, the Kingdom of God. In our present state as pilgrims we are at beta in the diagram above. At that stage our consciousness is not fully conscious, our reality not fully evolved into the new creature that we will be. Our consciousness reaches only to things that are at beta. We are not conscious of the reality of omega but grasp it merely in hope. Our consciousness participates in the character of beta. Beta is the region of things in need of transformation and redemption, hence the region of the unfinished. Things here are only half-being, that is, in process of becoming, and half-true. Symbolically, beta is the region of night and day, light and darkness. There is both a dark side to everything—that side that looks toward the future and is still unevolved—and a light side that looks to the present—that side that is already evolved, formed. Now, if Yahweh were to reveal himself at beta, he cannot come in his character as omega for that would mean the destruction of beta. Omega, you will recall, is the region of the fullness of being and of truth. So if omega suddenly appeared at the time beta it would mean the end of historical time, it would mean the "last times" or the end of the world. So for Yahweh to come to the region beta without putting a stop to the progress of beta toward omega, Yahweh has to hide himself, as it were, to take on the trappings of beta. This is the reason that when Yahweh appeared on Sinai and at the temple he veiled himself in a dense and dark cloud. This is the normal way in which Yahweh reveals himself, not the exceptional way. Yahweh is a hidden God and to express this mode of revelation the Old Testament writers and also the New Testament ones used the imagery of clouds.

In contrast to the biblical presentation of Yahweh as a hidden God is the Apollonian way which presents him as a reality which is always there, now and always.[5] He is expressed in the category of the Greek logos—light, being. In the Apollonian frame of reference, being is located at beta and so is light, for you will recall that for this philosophy the past and the future are nonbeing, hence formless, dark. Accordingly God was sought in the realm of beta and since the highest reality at beta is human consciousness, God was sought in human consciousness. Now the content of human consciousness are ideas so God was sought in the realm of ideas. Since God is the supreme reality and being so he must be expressed as the highest idea. We find the culmination of this theological enterprise in the Anselmian view of God as the Idea than which there is nothing greater. But God is not an Idea to be intuited nor is he arrived at by logical or discursive thought. God is not the conclusion of a syllogism. In short, God is not to be found in the realm of beta-consciousness. Why is this so? Because present or beta-consciousness is half-conscious, half-evolved, half-real, adequate for seeing objects at beta but not for grasping the reality of omega. Yahweh who is the Supremely Real and True cannot be present in a dimension which is only half-real and half-true. From this it does not follow that God is not in man, for the scriptures say that God is found in our most intimate depths. The most intimate depth of man, however, is not his consciousness but the region of the unconscious.

The unconscious you will recall is that dimension of man that looks toward the future. It is hidden from beta consciousness and therefore it appears dark. Because the unconscious has the dimension of the future in it, it is of a higher order of reality than beta consciousness. Just as the present is rooted in the future and derives its reality from it, so beta consciousness is rooted in the unconscious and derives its reality, power and ultimately its ideas from the unconscious. Now, Yahweh who is the Absolute Future, and therefore whose essential nature is future, if he is to be sought by man must be sought in the domain of the unconscious for it is the unconscious that participates in the character of the Absolute Future.

If Yahweh is in the region of the unconscious of the human psyche, then we can understand the scriptural description of him as a hidden God, whose abode is darkness and who manifests himself in dreams. Such imageries are not unusual or exceptional but the usual and normal way of describing the Israelite experience of the numinous and the divine.

But in the scriptures we also have the description of Yahweh as the Light in whom there is no darkness. How do we reconcile this expression with that other which speaks of him as dwelling in darkness? In the context of process thought there is no contradiction for the statements are made from different viewpoints or time dimensions. Thus, the symbolism of God as dwelling in darkness is valid as long as we take the present as vantage point, that is, the viewpoint of a pilgrim people, for the beta consciousness possessed by a pilgrim people looks at the Absolute Future as dark, for it is beyond the power of its light. When, however, the vantage point of the absolute or eschatological future is taken, then it is proper and necessary to describe it as the region of the fullness of light since light symbolizes the fullness of being and of truth. So when a prophet like John who was accorded a vision of God describes him as the Light in whom there is no darkness he was taking the standpoint of the eschaton.

The inability of Apollonian logic [6] to distinguish two levels of discourse in the scriptures, the apocalyptic and the historical, has led it to explain away the description of Yahweh as dwelling in darkness as an exception. Of course the Apollonian theologian would not say that this imagery is a contradiction for he believes that the scriptures are the word of God. But if he is faithful to his frame of meaning it is in fact a contradiction. It means that God is both good and evil, dwelling both in heaven and in hell, for darkness by the rules of his logic could have only a designation which does not contain its opposite. So if darkness has a negative designation it cannot also have a positive one. To say then that God is Light is necessarily to exclude the other imagery, namely, that he dwells in darkness. We have shown, however, that in a process frame of reference which allows for change and evolution there are various levels of discourse depending on the vantage point or time dimension. It is no contradiction, therefore, to say that God is Light and that he also dwells in darkness.

Let us now explain the process of spiritual transformation from the old Adam to the new which is symbolized in the scriptures as taking place at night and as a going back to the darkness of the womb in order to be reborn. Redemption as a rebirth means a metanoia, a change of heart. For the Christian this means having Faith and being baptized. Now Faith is not only the acceptance of truth in the logical and propositional sense but also the acceptance of a way of life as the true path, hence being true in one's life and actions. In contrast, lack of Faith is untruth or sin, which in the scriptures is expressed in the imagery of losing one's way, or, a missing of the mark. Again, the context is that of movement, process, travel. Truth is being on the right way to the Kingdom. It is within the context of travel or process that Christ's words, "I am the Way, the Truth and the Life," are to be understood. He is the Way to the land of truth and being.

Let us use again the diagram of process to illustrate the place and role of Faith in the religious life:

a	β	Ω
Unreason	Reason	Faith

Faith is situated at omega or the eschaton because for the Old and New Testament writers, revelation as the content of Faith is future, that is, it is a word of promise. As Johann B. Metz notes: [7]

> Most recent research has shown that the word of revelation in the Old Testament is not primarily a word of information or even a word of address, nor is it a word expressing the personal self-communication of God, but is rather a word of promise. . . . The principal word of promise points to the future; . . . in contrast to the Greeks for whom the world appears as a consistent and closed cosmos.

Metz elaborates by saying that "even the creation stories of the Old Testament are originally stories of promise, and faith in creation is faith in the promise." [8] In the New Testament, says Metz, "the forward-looking quality of biblical faith is in no way diminished," for "creative expectation is the secret essence of Christian existence in the New Testament." [9] We might add that Paul himself says that Faith is the substance of things hoped for, hence, it is a future reality.

Now, then, if Faith is situated in the eschaton, it follows that it appears dark to beta consciousness for as we noted earlier, beta consciousness has light to see only the objects at beta but is unable to peer into the eschatological future. The pilgrim people at beta live the night of Faith. This experience is expressed in the scriptures as the Passover night or the night of the Last Supper and is celebrated in the liturgy of the early Christians as a blessed night, a sacred night in which Yahweh is present but hidden. The memorialization and sacramental celebration of the Passover assures the guidance and salvific power of Yahweh such that there ensue a rebirth, a reaching of the Holy Land.

If to have Faith means union with Yahweh then it follows that one must be united with one's unconscious for it is here that Yahweh dwells. One must plunge into the dark depth of the unconscious. It is there that, to use the words and imagery of the scriptures, the Spirit hovers over the watery deep. To go back to the darkness of the unconscious is to go down to the waters of the Sea of Reeds or to go back to the darkness of the womb in order to be reborn. Just as the eschatological future is the womb of the historical present such that the possibilities of the present are realized, so the unconscious as the future dimension of the psyche is the womb from which beta consciousness is reborn to the dimension of Faith. The attainment of Faith is through the recovery of the archetypal symbols in the unconscious. But the recovery of the archetypal symbols requires that beta consciousness be quiescent, passive so that its thought and ideas do not prevent the surfacing of the archetypes. Then Yahweh is experienced as present, thanks to the mediation of the archetypes. This experience of Faith is expressed by the scriptures as Yahweh appearing at night in dreams. In other words, reason must be asleep, as it were, for it is not through its contents, namely, ideas, but through dreams, the content of the unconscious, that Yahweh is revealed.

The insight of the Israelites that through the archetypal symbols of the unconscious the numinous is revealed is no different from the insight of other cultures and peoples. As C. G. Jung has found from his lifelong work with peoples of both sexes and of different religions and cultures there are invariable archetypal symbols at the level of what he calls the collective unconscious which signify a deep desire of the soul to give birth to something new which is a process of liberation and individuation.[10] And Erich Neumann also notes that "the creative grace of renewal, healing and transformation, which emerges unexpectedly from the darkness of the unconscious, retains to the last its connection with the paradox of the *deus absconditus,* that unaccountable and inscrutably numinous power which may encounter the human ego under the guise of the Devil, the shadow of God, in the very citadel of the psyche." [11]

Apollonian theology which sees God only as Light would not think of directing those searching for God toward darkness for one must escape the dark cave of the unconscious to find God who is Light. The effort, however, has led to atheism and agnosticism for by the method of linguistic analysis which Apollonian culture has devised God is not an empirical reality verifiable in the present. If it is claimed by metaphysical theology that God is a metaphysical reality then it is incumbent upon it to discriminate between its formulation of God and false myths to show that its conception is not a false myth. Linguistic philosophy has shown however that metaphysical conceptions of God are meaningless. But linguistic analysis goes beyond its competence if it claims that there is no empirical basis for the reality of God.

Linguistic analysis is rooted in the Apollonian light-dark dualism. For it present consciousness is a light, not darkness, and present reality is the region of the empirical, that is, the real. But we already showed in a previous chapter that present or beta consciousness is a darkness in relation to its future state at omega. It does not have the power to verify all of reality for it is in a dimension of time which does not contain all of reality. God we showed is not at beta for this is the region of the unfinished, the half-evolved. So what it calls the empirical is not really empirical. The region of the empirical is at omega for it is there that things are fully real. But beta consciousness is not in that dimension. Therefore it cannot make a categorical assertion that all God-talk is meaningless.

Beta consciousness is a light in relation to objects in the present but paradoxically is darkness in relation to the reality of omega. It is the region of the unconscious which, because it participates in omega is the true light, while beta consciousness is darkness. It is in this sense that we may be able to understand the difficult saying of Jesus when he said that the light which is in one may be darkness. Thus he says: "But if your eye is diseased, your whole body will be all darkness. If then, the light inside you is darkness, what darkness that will be" (Mt. 6:23) and again: "See to it then that the light inside you is not darkness" (Lk. 11:35). Now light in the context of process thought is supposed to guide us toward the goal, in this case toward the Absolute Future, the eschaton. We have in our pilgrimage the light of reason or beta consciousness or the light of faith rooted in the unconscious. Without the light of faith, human reason cannot find the way to freedom and liberation. Human reason is indeed a light in the context of beta. It is able to know things at beta, to build a science and apply that science to the improvement and development of the world at beta. It can develop the method of linguistic analysis valid for determining meaning at beta. But the light of reason cannot show the way to the Land of Truth. To use the light of reason as the measure of what is real and true in an absolute way is idolatry. It leads to darkness in the negative signification of that term, that is, it leads to moral blindness, pride, sin. Hence the advice of Christ that we must see to it that we choose the proper light. The light of reason leads to negative darkness; the light of faith leads to redemption, liberation.

The light of faith appears as darkness to one who puts his faith in the light of reason alone. The content of Faith cannot be empirically verified by the method of reason; for it does not belong to the realm of beta consciousness. It derives from the unconscious. Hence Faith is a mystery to reason, a myth. Before the incomprehensible and dark the natural reaction of reason is first fear then incredulity, disbelief, denial. It will have no part of it for to do so would be the height of irrationality. The point of view of Faith precisely is that it is reason that is dark (negative sense), that it is unable to measure Faith, that when it calls Faith dark, mysterious, mere myth as opposed to objective truth, this is really a projection of its own dark condition. The point of view of Faith is that for reason to see it must first believe. This is of course a contradiction to reason, yet, the paradox is that it is in non-reason or in the unconscious that reason (beta consciousness) can find its truth. The paradox of Christianity is that what is wisdom to reason is foolishness to God and what seems foolish or irrational to reason is the true wisdom that leads to redemption. The darkness from which reason flees is the true path to truth and being. This is the constant teaching of the scriptures. The greatest redemptive acts in the history of salvation were done at night or in darkness: the first creation, the night of the Exodus, the night of the incarnation, the night of the Last Supper, the night of the resurrection. There is no other way to life, truth and being but through the positive darkness of Faith.

Alan Watts correctly criticizes Apollonian Christianity for not having come to terms with the dark side of human existence, with darkness as the bearer of Light. But his prescription is dubious for he suggests that one must embrace darkness personified as Lucifer. This is also the view of Erich Neumann who believes that God is composed of both positive and negative principles, hence goodness and evil.

The intentions of Watts and Neumann for remedying atheism and racism are laudable but their prescription can only bring greater chaos. They have failed to make a distinction between positive darkness and negative darkness, between a night that is sacred and blessed and a night that is accursed and calamitous. They see darkness only as negative (evil) which we have to embrace nevertheless in order to go beyond good and evil. Thus, they are still caught up in the Apollonian schema of things. The difference between their position and that of white theology is that while the latter prescribes a flight from all darkness as the way to freedom and liberation, theirs is a total embrace and acceptance of it.

The true dialectic of Christianity is from negative darkness to positive darkness. That this is the true dialectic is confirmed by none other than the recognized master of Christian mysticism, Dionysius the Areopagite.[12]

In the mystical theology of Dionysius, God is known as the Divine Darkness. Thus in the first chapter he says: [13]

Let this be my prayer; but do thou, dear Timothy, in the diligent exercise of mystical contemplation, leave behind the senses and the operations of the intellect, and all things sensible and intellectual, and all things in the world of being and non-being, that thou mayest arise, by Unknowing towards the union, as far as is attainable, with Him Who transcends all being and all knowledge. For by the unceasing and absolute renunciation of thyself and of all things, thou mayest be borne on high, through pure and entire self-abnegation, into the superessential Radiance of the Divine Darkness.

A commentary made by the editor properly notes for the reader that there are two main kinds of darkness: [14]

the sub-darkness and the super-darkness, between which lies, as it were, an octave of light. But the nether-darkness and the Divine Darkness are not the same darkness, for the former is absence of light, while the latter is excess of light. The one symbolizes mere Ignorance, and the other a transcendent "Unknowing"—a super-knowledge not obtained by means of the discursive reason.

Thus in mystical theology, darkness is a symbol not only of the negative but also and above all of the supremely positive—God. It is toward the Divine Darkness that man must tend and away from the sub-darkness or nether darkness of ignorance, sin, evil. The great religions as we have noted earlier always symbolized God as Darkness. And the editor of our text also notes that Damascius spoke of the ancient Egyptians as saying nothing about God, "but celebrated Him as a Darkness beyond all intellectual or spiritual perception,—a Thrice-Unknown Darkness." [15]

The mystical theology of Dionysius is known in the Christian tradition as negative theology. The great scholastic theologians knew about this negative theology. It is mentioned in the *Summa Theologiae* of St. Thomas.[16] But it was the rationalistic or Apollonian approach to the scriptures and theology that became dominant and within this frame of reference the method of negative theology could not be integrated. With the philosophy of process, however, it is possible to give a philosophic foundation for the ambivalent symbolism of darkness. Thus, Dionysius' mystical theology in which there are two levels of darkness is illustrated thus:

sub-darkness	light of reason	Super-Darkness
unconscious state of the material world	discursive knowledge	unconscious or "Unknowing"

In terms of the diagram, Western Apollonian theology was based on beta, that is, the dimension of reason. God became an Idea-than-which-there-was-nothing-greater or the supreme Being, hence symbolized by light, instead of being the beyond-Idea or the beyond-Being, hence, symbolized by Super-Darkness. The truer tradition is that of negative theology and Western Apollonian theology needs to recover it.[17] With this recovery, it is hoped that racism which ultimately derives from the Apollonian symbolism of black as wholly negative and white as wholly positive could be vanquished, at least at the intellectual level.

EPILOGUE

I hope that this work, conducted solely at the level of ideas, will be of some help at the level of action with regard to black-white relations. Ideas influence actions and vice versa. It is not necessary to determine which is prior. What is important is that we approach the problem of racism at both levels.

The counteracting of racism is not fully accomplished by concentrating our efforts on changing ways of life and behavior. Hence, the removal of economic, political and cultural inequalities though important and most urgent is not enough to combat racism. Nor do I believe that once the economic, political and social inequalities are resolved that belief will follow practice. There is an intellectual and ideational dimension to racism that is impervious to practice, therefore liberation must also take place at the level of mind and idea.

A negative self-image on the part of one and an inflated self-image on the part of the other are equally destructive of the possessors of such images. White Christianity, as we have shown, has been partly responsible for the false images possessed by both blacks and whites due to its one-sided color symbolism, hence, it is the task of Christianity to help eliminate this ideational dimension of racism.

As a Christian I was interested to know if the Faith I was brought up in and follow was intrinsically racistic or not. Hence, this was partly the reason for undertaking the present study. But another reason was the fact that many blacks were giving up on Christianity since they equated it with white or Apollonian Christianity. Western theologians have not done much to show that Christian theology itself is not racistic. They have merely insisted that God created all men equal and loves them all equally. But this intellectual belief has not influenced very much the actions of white Christians toward dark-skinned peoples and black Christians toward their own selves, for undercutting that belief is the symbolism supposedly based on the authority of the Bible that black is associated with sin and the devil and white with goodness and God. No amount of intellectual persuasion that the transference of the symbolism to skin color is invalid will prevent the transference and association. The only solution is to show that on the authority of the Bible black is a positive symbol— the symbol of the divine and of goodness.

FOOTNOTES

INTRODUCTION

1 We hope to show the importance of the imagination for theology in a future work.

2 I make a distinction in this study between white theology and white Christianity, on the one hand, and Western theology and Western Christianity, on the other. White theology is a brand of Western theology. The other branch of Western theology is what is known as negative theology. While white theology is rationalistic and conceptual, negative theology is mystical and symbolic. My quarrel is not with Western theology and Western Christianity as such but with a particular brand of it, namely, white theology and white Christianity. It is the black-white color symbolism of white theology and the application of it to race relations by white Christianity that are partly the cause of racism in the West. Because this symbolism became dominant in the Christian West, I feel justified in calling it the Western color symbolism. In the course of my study, then, I shall use the terms white theology and white Christianity interchangeably, and when I speak of the Western color symbolism, I mean the symbolism as found in white theology and white Christianity.

CHAPTER 1

1 For the source of these several studies on color symbolism I depend on the article of Kenneth J. Gergen, "The Significance of Skin Color in Human Relations," *Color and Race,* ed. J. H. Franklin (Boston: Beacon Press, 1968), p. 119. Originally published in *Daedalus, Color and Race,* 1967. Copyright © 1967 by American Academy of Arts and Sciences.

2 *Loc. cit.* As far as the Afro-Americans are concerned, their negative attitude toward the color black could be attributed to Westernization. There are those, however, who would maintain that the color black is a natural negative symbol. Gergen, for one, holds to this view. We will have occasion in the course of the study to deal with this issue.

[3] See his book, *The Luminous Darkness* (New York: 1965), pp. 59-60.

[4] P. J. Heather, "Colour Symbolism," *Folklore*, 59 (1948), p. 168.

[5] *Ibid.*, p. 169.

[6] *Loc. cit.*

[7] *Ibid.*, p. 170.

[8] See his article, "Blackness and Whiteness," *Encounter*, 21 (1963), pp. 12-13.

[9] Thurman, *op. cit.*, pp. 59-60.

[10] Bastide, *op. cit.*, pp. 36-37.

[11] See his book, *Bible Themes* (Notre Dame: Fides, 1964), Vol. II, p. 161.

[12] The reader should not jump to the conclusion based on the passages to be examined that the scriptures themselves are inherently dualistic and racistic for the passages presented in this chapter are the ones chosen by white theology to prove its claim that in the scriptures black or darkness as a negative symbol and white or light as a positive one are the rule, not the exception.

In a later chapter I will attempt to show a more objective reading of the scriptures with regard to the color symbolism of black and white. For the present let me note that frequency of use or occurrence should not be the criterion used for determining the color symbolisms of black and white. The more objective criterion is the degree of importance of the object symbolized. It is the object symbolized that gives the true meaning and importance to the symbol. If the object symbolized is a central category in the scriptures and is a primary reality in the redemptive process, then this fact should be given greater weight than a comparative and statistical count of passages.

[13] See also Amos 8:0; 5:8, 18-20; Isa. 13:9-10.

[14] "Plunged into darkness" is a variable reading of "scattered."

[15] See also Ps. 17:29.

[16] See also John 12:35-36.

[17] See also Isa. 2:5; 2 Cor. 6:14-16; Matt. 5:13-16.

[18] See also Matt. 22:13.

[19] See also John 12:46-47; Isa. 9:1-6.

[20] See also 1 Pet. 2:8-10; John 3:17-21.

[21] See also Acts 13:46-47; 26:22-23.

[22] See also Mark 4:21-25; Matt. 25:1-30.

[23] See also 1 Thess. 5:2-7; Apoc. 22:4-5; Rom. 13:12; Isa. 60:1-20.

[24] See also Gen. 1:3-5; 8:22; Jer. 33:19-26; Job 5:14.

[25] See also Judges 20:33; 1 Kings 15:11; Ps. 21:3; 41:4; 76:3.

[26] See also John 9:3; 13:30; Apoc. 21:25; 22:5.

[27] See Isa. 17:14; 50:10; Ps. 16:3; 29:6; 58:7; 87:10; 106:10.

[28] See also Soph. 3:5; Ps. 5:4; 129:6; 142:8; John 8:12.

[29] See also 4 Kings 4:31; Isa. 26:19; Ps. 151:10.

[30] See Ex. 11:4; 12:8-12; Wis. 17:2-20; 18:1-14: Rom. 13:11-14.

[31] See also Ex. 14:20-21; Ps. 104:39.

[32] See also Isa. 1:18.

[33] Ecc. 9:8.

[34] See *The Oxford Concise Concordance,* ed. Bruce Metzger and Isobel Metzger (New York: Oxford Univ. Press, 1962), p. 150. See also, Rev. 3:4, 4:4, 15:6; Matt. 28:3.

[35] See *Harper's Topical Concordance,* ed. Charles R. Joy (rev. ed., New York: Harper & Brothers, 1940), p. 64.

[36] See P. J. Heather, *op. cit.,* p. 169.

[37] See Lam. 5:10; Jer. 8:21; Rev. 6:12; Job 3:5; Jer. 4:28.

[38] See also Ecc. 6:12; Ps. 102:11.

CHAPTER 2

[1] See Leon Carl Brown, "Color in Northern Africa," in *Color and Race,* p. 189.

[2] See Talcott Parsons, "The Problem of Polarization on the Axis of Color," *Color and Race,* p. 366. See also George Kelsey, *Racism and the Christian Understanding of Man* (Quoted from *Philosophy for a New Generation,* ed. A. Bierman & J. Gould (Macmillan, 1970), p. 265.

[3] See his masterful study, *White Over Black* (Chapel Hill: University of North Carolina Press and Institute of Early American History and Culture, © 1968); all quotes and references to this book are taken from the paperback edition by Penguin Books, Inc., Baltimore, 1968; for this quote, see p. 7.

[4] Quoted from Jordan, *op. cit.,* p. 7.

[5] *Loc. cit.*

[6] *Loc. cit.*

[7] *Loc. cit.*

[8] Leon Carl Brown, *op. cit.,* p. 191.

[9] *Loc. cit.*

[10] *Loc. cit.*

[11] Jordan, *op. cit.,* p. 4.

[12] *Loc. cit.*

[13] *Ibid.,* p. 6.

[14] *Ibid.,* p. 17. Also discrediting the theory was the experience of Englishmen that though the complexion was darkened by prolonged stay in the tropics, the return to cooler climates would restore the original color.

[15] *Ibid.,* pp. 17-18.

[16] *Ibid.,* p. 18.

[17] *Loc. cit.*

[18] *Ibid.,* p. 37.

[19] *Loc. cit.*

[20] *Loc. cit.*

[21] *Loc. cit.*

[22] See Arrah B. Evarts, "Color Symbolism," *Psychoanalytic Review,* 6 (1919), p. 131.

The devotion to the Black Madonna in the Middle Ages might be adduced as contradicting our position that Mary was Aryanized. The devotion to the Black Madonna, in my view, traces its beginings to very early times, when mysticism and negative theology were still quite dominant. Thus, black, in this tradition was seen as positive and as a symbol of the divine. (We shall amply document this assertion in the latter part of our study.) But with the triumph of rational theology, devotion to the Black Virgin began to be explained as an aberration in which black now symbolized magic and sorcery. Thus as Bastide notes (*ibid.*, p. 38):

> The Black Virgin represents to her devotees not so much the Loving Mother as a sorceress, a rain maker, a worker of miracles. She has the magnetism of the strange, magic,—even a near-diabolical sorcery—were involved in her miracles. She is not the beloved mother who clasps the unfortunate to her white breast and comforts them with her milky white arms, drying their childish tears with the fair tresses of her bright-colored hair, but a mysterious goddess endowed with extraordinary powers. The symbolism of her dark color is not eliminated in the cult; it is only repressed—and badly repressed—because it infiltrates into the prayers that are directed toward her. Nevertheless, the Black Virgin helps one to understand the appeal used by Catholicism in its efforts to convert pagan peoples to the faith.

[23] Evarts, p. 130.
[24] Bastide, p. 38.
[25] *Loc. cit.*
[26] Evarts, p. 130.
[27] Bastide, p. 38.
[28] *Ibid.*, p. 39.
[29] *Ibid.*, p. 39.
[30] *Loc. cit.*
[31] *Loc. cit.*
[32] Jordon, *op. cit.*, p. 41.
[33] *Loc. cit.*
[34] *Loc. cit.*
[35] *Ibid.*, p. 40.
[36] *Loc. cit.*
[37] *Ibid.*, p. 41.
[38] *Ibid.*, p. 40.
[39] *Ibid.*, p. 40-41.
[40] *Ibid.*, p. 41.
[41] *Loc. cit.*
[42] *Ibid.*, p. 42.
[43] *Loc. cit.*
[44] See his book, *Soul on Ice* (New York: Delta Books, 1968), p. 160.
[45] *Loc. cit.*
[46] *Ibid.*, p. 161.
[47] *Ibid.*, p. 159.

172   *Footnotes*

[48] *Ibid.*, pp. 159-60.
[49] Bastide, *op. cit.*, p. 43.
[50] *Ibid.*, p. 44.
[51] *Loc. cit.*
[52] *Loc. cit.*
[53] Gergen, *op. cit.*, p. 115.
[54] For the purpose of correcting religious practices influenced by Western color symbolism, a more detailed study than the one made here is in order. Speaking of reform in religious practice, may I suggest that in Catholic churches blonde statues and pictures of Jesus and Mary be removed not only in the interest of historical accuracy (Semites were dark-skinned people) but in the interest of counteracting the ill effects of Western color symbolism. For those who consider skin color in these statues a small matter (for they do not affect the "substance" of the Faith), then the change should not be too difficult. But my guess is that for the many the suggested change is not a small matter, for these blonde statues represent an underlying symbolism of color that colors (excuse the pun) their Christian consciousnesses. If this is true, then there is all the more reason for a change, in order to make Christianity the universal religion which it claims to be.

CHAPTER 3

[1] See his article, "Symbolic Color in Literature of the English Renaissance," *Philological Quarterly*, 15 (1936), p. 81.
[2] *Ibid.*, p. 83. He cites Spenser's *Faerie Queene*, III, xii, 1612: "black boure of sorrowe" and grief clad in sable.
[3] *Ibid.*, p. 88. See *F.Q.*, V, ix, 3112; *Epithalamion*, p. 151.
[4] See his "Blackness and Whiteness," in *Encounter*, 21 (1936), p. 13.
[5] *Ibid.*, p. 13. See also *Macbeth*, "The devil damn thee black." In *Titus Andronicus*, the villain is a black man.
[6] See her book, *Shakespeare's Imagery* (Cambridge University Press, 1961), pp. 64-65.
[7] *Romeo and Juliet*, 3.2.18.
[8] Spurgeon, *op. cit.*, p. 64.
[9] *Op. cit.*, p. 38.
[10] *Op. cit.*, p. 175.
[11] *Ibid.*, p. 176-177.
[12] See Harry Levin, *The Power of Blackness* (New York, 1960).
[13] *Op. cit.*, p. 14.
[14] H. Isaacs, *op. cit.*, p. 14.
[15] See Evarts, *op. cit.*, p. 134; Heather, *op. cit.*, p. 176.
[16] Bastide, *op. cit.*, p. 44.
[17] *Loc. cit.*
[18] See his well-known work, *The Protestant Ethic and the Spirit of Capitalism*, trans. T. Parsons (New York: Charles Scribner's Sons, 1958).
[19] *Ibid.*, p. 105.

[20] *Ibid.*, pp. 105, 117.

[21] *Ibid.*, p. 105.

[22] *Ibid.*, pp. 114-115.

[23] *Ibid.*, pp. 121, 125, 154.

[24] *Ibid.*, pp. 161-62.

[25] *Loc. cit.*

[26] *Ibid.*, p. 163.

[27] The Puritan ethic, of course, is much more than just a justification of labor and profit as pleasing to God. Our concern here, however, is the theological color symbolism of black and white applied to the economic relation of white and black peoples.

[28] *Op. cit.*, p. 48.

[29] Weber, *op. cit.*, pp. 48-49.

[30] *Ibid.*, p. 53.

[31] *Ibid.*, pp. 53-54.

[32] William H. Marnell, *Man-Made Morals* (New York: Anchor Books, 1968), pp. 24-43.

[33] *Ibid.*, p. 242.

[34] *Ibid.*, p. 245.

[35] *Ibid.*, pp. 245-246.

[36] *Ibid.*, p. 251.

[37] *Essays of William Graham Sumner*, ed. A. G. Keller and M. R. Davie, 2 vols. (New Haven: Yale University Press, 1940), I, p. 301. Quoted from William Marnell, *op. cit.*, pp. 251-52.

[38] Quoted from John Kenneth Galbraith's *The Affluent Society* (New York: Mentor Books, 1968), p. 56.

[39] *Loc. cit.*

[40] Marnell, *op. cit.*, p. 258.

[41] *Ibid.*, p. 354.

[42] *Ibid.*, p. 355.

[43] *Op. cit.*, p. 47.

[44] *Ibid.*, pp. 47-48.

CHAPTER 4

[1] See Norman Brown, *Life Against Death* (Wesleyan Univ. Press, 1959), p. x.

[2] *The Little Black Boy* by William Blake. Quoted from Harold Isaacs, *op. cit.*, p. 14.

[3] Maud Ballington Booth, *Sleepy-Time Stories* (New York, 1900). Quoted from Harold Isaacs, *op. cit.*, p. 15.

[4] Brown, *op. cit.*, p. 4.

[5] Publ. by New American Library, 1947.

[6] See his well-known work on the psychopathology of blackness, *Black Skin, White Masks* (New York: Grove Press, Inc., 1967), p. 187.

[7] Fanon notes that Jung locates the collective unconscious in the inherited cerebral matter. But for Fanon, the collective unconscious "is

purely the sum of prejudices, myths, collective attitudes of a given group." (See Fanon, *op. cit.,* p. 188). The difference is not unimportant, for according to Jung, the same psychic structure as the white man's is also found in nonwhites (*ibid.,* p. 187). Fanon believes, however, that the similarity is due to traumatic contacts with the white man (*loc. cit.* and p. 191).

8 *Ibid.,* p. 189.

9 See his book, *White Racism* (New York: Pantheon Books, 1970), p. 232.

10 *Ibid.,* p. 233.

11 *Ibid.,* p. 239.

12 *Loc. cit.*

13 *Ibid.,* pp. 116-17.

14 *Ibid.,* p. 233.

15 *Loc. cit.*

16 *Ibid.,* p. 240.

17 See his *Depth Psychology and a New Ethic,* trans. Eugene Rolfe (New York: G. P. Putnam's Sons, 1969).

18 *Ibid.,* p. 51.

19 *Ibid.,* p. 45.

20 *Loc. cit.*

21 *Ibid.,* p. 52.

22 *Ibid.,* p. 55.

23 *Ibid.,* p. 56.

24 *Loc. cit.*

25 *Ibid.,* p. 25.

26 From "*Playboy* Interview: Marshall McLuhan," *Playboy* Magazine, March, 1969, p. 66.

27 Harold Isaacs, "Group Identity and Political Change," in *Color and Race,* p. 81.

28 Fanon, *op. cit.,* p. 154.

29 *Ibid.,* pp. 147-48.

30 *Ibid.,* p. 146.

31 *Loc. cit.*

32 *Ibid.,* p. 152.

33 *Op. cit.,* p. 46.

34 *Op. cit.,* p. 121.

35 *Ibid.,* pp. 121-22.

36 *Ibid.,* p. 122.

37 See his article, "Blackness and Whiteness," in *Encounter,* 21 (August, 1963), p. 12.

38 *Ibid.,* p. 125.

39 *Ibid.,* p. 125.

40 *Op. cit.,* p. 39.

41 *Loc. cit.*

42 *Ibid.,* p. 40.

43 Published by Sheed and Ward, Inc., 1968.

44 *Ibid.,* p. 111.

[45] Published by The Seabury Press, New York, 1969.
[46] See E. U. Essien-Udom, *Black Nationalism* (Chicago, Univ. of Chicago Press, 1962), p. 6.
[47] *Ibid.,* p. 7, fn.
[48] *Ibid.,* p. 6.

CHAPTER 5

[1] *Op. cit.,* p. 129.
[2] *Loc. cit.*
[3] *Op. cit.,* pp. 129-130.
[4] *Op. cit.,* pp. 119-120.
[5] See his article, "The Social Perception of Skin Color in Japan," *Color and Race,* ed. J. H. Franklin (Boston: Beacon Press, 1968), p. 129.
[6] *Loc. cit.*
[7] *Ibid.,* p. 130.
[8] *Ibid.,* p. 132.
[9] See his article, "Race and Descent as Social Categories in India," *Color and Race,* p. 173.
[10] *Ibid.,* p. 166.
[11] *Op. cit.,* p. 14, fn. 4.
[12] Gergen, *op. cit.,* p. 118.
[13] *Loc. cit.*
[14] *Loc. cit.*
[15] See his book, *The Masks of God: Primitive Mythology* (New York: Viking Press, 1959), pp. 57-58.
[16] *Op. cit.,* p. 120.
[17] See Thierry Maertens, *Bible Themes,* II (Bruges: Biblica, 1964), p. 451.
[18] Campbell, *op. cit.,* p. 66.
[19] *Ibid.,* pp. 65-66.
[20] Campbell states: "The state of the child in the womb is one of bliss, actionless bliss, and this state may be compared to the beatitude visualized for paradise. In the womb, the child is unaware of the alternation of night and day, or of any of the images of temporality. It should not be surprising, therefore, if the metaphors used to represent eternity suggest, to those trained in symbolism of the infantile unconscious, retreat to the womb." *Ibid.,* p. 65.
[21] From the *Mythology of All Races,* vol. 12, pp. 94, 97, 413. (Quoted from Rev. J. W. Marcel, *God, The Bible and the Black Liberation Struggle* (Washington Institute of Black History and Religion, Washington, D.C.), p. 36.
[22] See his *Anacalypsis,* Vol. I, p. 286. (Quoted from J. A. Rogers, *Sex and Race,* I (N.Y.: Helga M. Rogers, 9th ed., 1967), p. 266.
[23] *Ibid.* Quoted from J. Rogers, *op. cit.,* p. 332.
[24] The rational process can be seen in Plato who made an effort to

rationalize the Greek religions and myths, deemphasizing the artistic and imaginative dimensions of experience, and emphasizing the rational.

25 See J. Rogers, *op. cit.,* p. 265.

26 *Ibid.,* pp. 265-266.

27 *Ibid.,* p. 266.

28 *Ibid.,* p. 270.

29 *Ibid.,* p. 272.

30 *Ibid.,* p. 270.

31 See John S. Mbiti, *Concepts of God in Africa* (New York: Praeger Publishers, 1970), pp. 154-55.

32 *Ibid.,* p. 155.

33 *Ibid.,* p. 154.

34 *Ibid.,* p. 155.

35 *Loc. cit.*

36 See the studies of Lucien Lévy-Bruhl in his books, *How Natives Think* (N.Y.: Washington Square Press, 1966) and *Primitive Mentality* (Boston: Beacon Press, 1966).

37 See J. A. Rogers, *op. cit.,* p. 274.

38 *Loc. cit.*

39 *Loc. cit.*

40 *Loc. cit.*

41 *Ibid.,* p. 275.

42 *Loc. cit.*

43 *Loc. cit.*

44 See *Mystical Theology of Dionysius the Areopagite* (London: The Shrine of Wisdom, 1923), p. 5.

45 P. J. Heather, *op. cit.,* p. 175-177.

46 *Op. cit.,* p. 131.

CHAPTER 6

1 This type of mentality is not confined to professional scientists and technicians but is present also among theologians, philosophers, artists, etc.

2 See Erich Neumann, *The Great Mother,* An Analysis of the Archetype, (New York: Pantheon Books, Inc., 1955), p. xlii.

3 *Ibid.,* p. xliii.

4 All we need do here to show the ambivalence of darkness is show the positive darkness of mythic experience, since for rational man myth and the unconscious are already experienced negatively.

5 The term primal or early man does not mean undeveloped, inferior, primitive, prelogical or other such derogatory terms. After all early man has something that modern man is trying to recover, viz., mythic experience, so necessary for psychic wholeness.

6 *Op. cit.,* pp. 16-17.

7 *Ibid.,* p. 16.

[8] See his book, *Civilization in Transition*, pp. 144-45. (Quoted from Joseph Campbell, *The Masks of God: Creative Mythology* [New York: Viking Press, 1968], p. 645.)

[9] Quoted from Campbell, *op. cit.*, p. 656.

[10] *Ibid.*, pp. 647-48.

[11] *Ibid.*, p. 656.

[12] See Lucien Lévy Bruhl, *How Natives Think* (Washington Square Press), p. 63.

[13] *Ibid.*, p. 64.

[14] *Loc. cit.*

[15] They see a mystic oneness with nature. Thus tribes feel that they are themselves but also are identical with their totems. For example, "the Trumai (a tribe of Northern Brazil) say that they are aquatic animals.—The Bororo (a neighbouring tribe) boast that they are red araras (parakeets)." (See *How Natives Think*, p. 62).

[16] *How Natives Think*, p. 24.

[17] *Ibid.*, p. 31.

[18] *Loc. cit.*

[19] *Ibid.*, p. 25.

[20] Says Lévy-Bruhl, "It is of the very essence of participation that all idea of duality is effaced, and that in spite of the law of contradiction the subject is at the same time himself and the being in whom he participates." (*How Natives Think*, p. 345.)

[21] *Ibid.*, p. 27.

[22] *Ibid.*, p. 42.

[23] *Ibid.*, p. 43.

[24] McLuhan, to be sure, is not without his faults. He exaggerates the principle "the medium is the message" as a universal principle of explanation. This is reductionism which fallacy was not avoided either by Marx or by Freud. But just as the reductionisms of the latter do not detract from their fundamental insights, so it is the case with McLuhan.

[25] See "*Playboy Interview:* Marshall McLuhan," *Playboy* Magazine, March, 1969, p. 59.

[26] *Loc. cit.*

[27] *Loc. cit.*

[28] *Loc. cit.*

[29] *Ibid.*, p. 64.

[30] *Ibid.*, p. 66.

[31] *Ibid.*, p. 72.

[32] *Ibid.*, p. 70.

[33] See his *Feast of Fools* (Cambridge: Harvard U. Press, 1969), p. 15.

[34] Kovel, *op. cit.*, p. 235.

[35] Neumann, *Depth Psychology and a New Ethic*, p. 9.

[36] See his book, *Life Against Death* (Wesleyan Univ. Press, 1959), p. 175.

[37] *Ibid.*, p. 174.

[38] *Ibid.*, p. 175.

³⁹ *Ibid.,* p. 174.

⁴⁰ *Op. cit.,* pp. 120-21.

⁴¹ Quoted from Gergen, *op. cit.,* p. 121.

⁴² *Ibid.,* p. 121.

⁴³ See Bastide, *op. cit.,* p. 119.

⁴⁴ See Alexander Thomas and Samuel Sillen, *Racism and Psychiatry* (New York: Brunner/Mazel, 1972), Ch. 7 "The Sexual Mystique." See also Eldridge Cleaver, *Soul on Ice,* pp. 155-190.

⁴⁵ Thomas and Sillen, *op. cit.,* p. 102.

CHAPTER 7

¹ See his *From Religion to Philosophy,* pp. 242-261. Cornford notes, e.g., that in the *Timaeus* we have a mythic cosmology. But "if Plato could have stated it as a *logos,* he would have done so, only too gladly" (p. 261-62). Cornford uses the terms "scientific" and "mystical" for Apollonian and Dyonisian (p. vi). It was the former that triumphed in Greek philosophic thought—the effort to remove all that was vague and mythical in religion (p. 261).

² See his *Chance, Love, and Logic* (New York: George Braziller, Inc., 1956), pp. 267-300.

³ The process philosophy presented here takes its inspiration from Teilhard de Chardin who in my mind has been able to combine not only in his own person but also in his writings both the Apollonian and the Dionysian dimensions of Western culture.

⁴ *Op. cit.,* p. 199.

⁵ Opinion of a judge by the name of Tom P. Brady. Quoted from James G. Cook, *The Segregationists* (New York, 1962), p. 17.

⁶ Opinion of a physician. Quoted from Allison Davis, Burleigh B. Gardner and Mary R. Gardner, *Deep South* (Chicago: University of Chicago Press, 1941), pp. 16-17.

⁷ *Timaeus,* 37d.

⁸ *Enneads,* 3:7,7; 3:7,11.

⁹ *Physics* IV, 222b.

¹⁰ *Ibid.,* 221a.

¹¹ Past and future here mean absolute past and future, i.e., first beginnings and last end.

¹² For a fuller description of a philosophy of process, see my book, *Teilhard and the Supernatural* (Baltimore: Helicon Press, 1966), Part Two.

¹³ See his book, *Depth Psychology and a New Ethic,* trans. Eugene Rolfe (New York: G. P. Putnam's Sons, 1969), pp. 143-44.

¹⁴ See his book, *Myth and Ritual in Christianity* (Boston: Beacon Press, 1968), p. 18.

CHAPTER 8

¹ Let us reserve our judgment on what the primary and secondary symbolism of darkness or blackness in the scriptures is until we have

examined the passages that use darkness as a positive symbol.

[2] See also Gen. 40:11 which contains the account of God communicating with Pharaoh in a dream. See also Gen. 31:11, 28; No. 22:8-20.

[3] The term redemption here means buying back the field of Elimelech (Ruth's deceased husband) and raising up children to him. These are the duties of Boaz or whoever was the closest relative of the deceased.

[4] As David Stanley notes: "Because they were accustomed to consider cosmic origins as the beginning of salvation-history, the later OT writers found it quite natural to express the eschatological salvation of the 'last times,' the climax of Yahweh's interventions on behalf of His chosen people, as a second and more marvelous creation." See his "The New Testament Doctrine of Baptism," *Theological Studies*, 18 (1957), p. 179.

[5] In mythologies of most cultures, night is given priority over day, for night is seen as the mother of day. See E. Neumann, *The Great Mother* (New York: Pantheon Books, Inc., 1955), p. 56.

[6] *Ibid.*, p. 179.

[7] *Ibid.*, pp. 179-80.

[8] The Sea of Reeds. Whether there was actually a sea or not is immaterial for our purpose. It is the symbolism behind the symbol that interests us, regardless of whether the symbol is a historical reality or not.

[9] As David Stanley notes: "What is true of OT literature holds good also for that of the NT, in which the creation theme is pressed into the service of soteriology. In fact, it may be asserted that the concept of the "new creation," together with its counterpart, the idea of regeneration or birth anew, forms the most apt expression of the salvation revealed in Jesus." *Op cit.*, p. 180.

The imagery of rebirth always points to the image of the womb. Rebirth is symbolized as a return to the darkness of the womb, hence, darkness or night is the most apt symbol of creativity, regeneration, redemption.

[10] See also 1 Thess. 5:2.

[11] See also Matt. 19:28; John 3:3ff; Eph. 2:4-6; 1 John *passim;* 1 Pt. 1:3, 23; 2:2.

[12] We do not deny the symbolism of God as light in the scriptures, but what needs to be brought out is that God is also symbolized by darkness and his presence by clouds.

[13] See Ex. 40:34-36; Num. 19:15-22; Deut. 5:22; 2 Par. 7:1-2; Isa. 6:1-7, etc.

[14] *Op. cit.*, vol. I, p. 252.

[15] See also Matt. 24:30-31; Mk. 13:26; 14:62; Lk. 9:34-35; 21:27; Apoc. 1:7; 14:14-16; 1 Thess. 4:17.

[16] See also 2 Pt. 1:17-19; Ex. 19:16; Ps. 96:2; 103:3.

[17] *Op. cit.*, vol. 1, p. 51.

[18] *Loc. cit.*

[19] See Job. 30:30; Lm. 4:8.

CHAPTER 9

[1] John L. McKenzie, S.J., *Dictionary of the Bible* (Milwaukee: Bruce, 1965), p. 175.

[2] For a more detailed explanation of the eschatological future, see my book, *God Within Process* (Newman Press, 1970), Introduction.

[3] See his *The Theology of Hope* (New York: Harper & Row, 1967), pp. 16-17.

[4] See his article, "Creative Hope," *Cross Currents,* 17 (1967), p. 174.

[5] Moltmann, *op. cit.,* pp. 16-17.

[6] Aristotelian metaphysical philosophy is inadequate as a frame of reference for understanding the scriptures which are historical and apocalyptic in nature. Both historical and apocalyptic discourses are within the context of time, historical time or eschatological time. Eternity in biblical thought is the fullness of time or unending time, not timelessness. Metaphysical discourse is timeless discourse, supposedly to free us from false myths but, ironically, it has led us down the path of false myths.

[7] *Op. cit.,* p. 173.

[8] *Loc. cit.*

[9] *Ibid.,* p. 174.

[10] Cf. his *Psychology of Religion* (Yale, 1938), pp. 1-77. Cf. also Ira Progoff, *Jung's Psychology and Social Meaning* (New York: Julian Press, 1953), pp. 90-93, 194-97, 208-213.

[11] *Op. cit.,* p. 146.

[12] It has never been ascertained who is the real author of the theological treatises known as the *Corpus Areopagiticum.* But the authority of the treatises is unquestioned for it was held in high esteem not only by mystics but by Popes and professional theologians like Albert the Great and Thomas Aquinas.

[13] *Mystical Theology of Dionysius the Areopagite* (London: The Shrine of Wisdom, 1923), p. 5.

[14] *Loc. cit.* Comment 1.

[15] *Loc. cit.,* Comment 2.

[16] See, e.g., *S.T.,* 12 and 13; *Contra Gentiles,* 1,14.

[17] This has been the insistent thesis of Joseph Campbell, one of the foremost authorities on mythology in the West, in his many books on mythology. For him the mystical tradition of Eckhart, John Tauler, Suso and Ruysbroeck is the truer tradition than the official theology of the Church (See *Occidental Mythology,* p. 515). He notes further that the alienation of Western man which Marx, Freud and the existentialists have noted is due to the loss of the sense of myth and that the rationalization and demythologization process in theology resulting in the secularization of the sacred is a step in the wrong direction. See *The Flight of the Wild Gander* (N.Y.: The Viking Press, 1951), pp. 222-226.